Mastering
REFERRALS
Book 7
8 Books to 8 Figures Series

Jason Miller

ISBN: 978-1-957217-57-4 (hardcover)
ISBN: 978-1-957217-58-1 (paperback)
ISBN: 978-1-957217-59-8 (ebook)

TABLE OF CONTENTS

INTRODUCTION

Referral programs are a game-changer for businesses. At its core, a referral program is a system that rewards people for recommending your products or services to others. The main players in a referral program are the referrers, the people who make the recommendations; the incentives, which are the rewards given for successful referrals; and the tracking system that ensures referrals are properly recorded and rewarded.

Referral programs have been around in some form for a long time. Originally, word-of-mouth was the go-to method. People naturally recommended businesses they liked to their friends and family. However, as businesses grew and markets became more competitive, word-of-mouth evolved into more structured programs. Companies realized that they could tap into a powerful marketing tool by formalizing these recommendations. So, they began to create systems that encouraged referrals, tracked them, and provided rewards. This evolution transformed casual recommendations into a strategic part of many business models.

The data on referral programs is impressive. Studies show that customers who come through referrals tend to be more loyal and have a higher lifetime value than those who come through other channels. For instance, one study found that referred customers have a 16 percent higher lifetime value. Another report highlighted that referral programs can generate up to 5 times more sales than paid advertising. These statistics underscore the effectiveness of referral programs and their ability to drive sustainable growth. Different industries have also seen varied success rates. In the tech industry, referral programs are especially popular, with some companies attributing up to 50 percent of their new customer acquisitions to referrals. In retail, referral programs have boosted sales by 20 to 30 percent.

By understanding what a referral program is, its history, and the data supporting its effectiveness, we can appreciate why it's such a vital tool for businesses. As we move through this book, we'll explore how to set up and optimize your referral program, ensuring it becomes a key driver of your business success.

Let me tell you a story about a time when a referral program changed everything for a client of mine. This client ran a small marketing firm. Business was steady, but growth was slow. She was looking for a way to bring in more clients without spending a fortune on advertising. We talked about various options, and I suggested she try a referral program.

At first, she was hesitant. She wasn't sure if her clients would be interested in referring others, and she didn't know how to set up the program. But she decided to give it a shot. We sat down and worked out the details. She offered a discount on future services to any client who referred a new customer. We also set up a simple tracking system to ensure she could see where the referrals were coming from and reward the clients who made them.

Within a month, she saw a noticeable increase in new clients. One of her existing clients, who was very happy with her services, referred three new businesses in just two weeks. This client was thrilled to receive the discount on her next project, and the new clients were excited to work with someone who came so highly recommended. This created a win-win situation. My client's business started to grow faster, and she didn't have to spend extra money on traditional advertising.

The key moments in this story were when the first few referrals came in, and my client saw the immediate benefits. She realized that her clients were not only willing to refer others but were happy to do so, especially when they received something in return. This was a turning point for her business.

From this experience, I learned that a well-structured referral program can be a powerful tool for growth. It's not just about getting new clients; it's about building a network of loyal customers who actively promote your business. The success of my client's program showed me that when people are satisfied with your service and have an incentive to spread the word, they will.

This story ties into the book's broader theme: the importance of creating systems that benefit everyone involved. Referral programs work because they create a cycle of positive reinforcement. Clients feel appreciated and rewarded, new customers come in with trust already built, and businesses grow more sustainably. This book will guide you through setting up your referral program so you, too, can experience these benefits.

As we dive into this book, I want to give you a clear picture of what to expect and how best to use the information here. We'll explore referral programs from every angle, making sure you have all the tools and insights needed to create a program that works for your business.

In the first chapter, we'll start with the basics. You'll learn what a referral program is, why it's important, and how it can benefit your business. We'll look at the key components that make up a successful referral program and go through some historical context to show how these programs have evolved over time.

Next, in Chapter Two, we'll discuss the triangle principle, which is all about creating a win-win-win scenario. You'll see how this principle can guide your business decisions and ensure that everyone involved in the referral process benefits. I'll share examples and strategies to help you implement this approach in your business.

Chapter Three will focus on setting up your referral program. We'll go step-by-step through the process of identifying potential referrers, setting up incentives, and creating a tracking system. You'll learn how to build a community of brand ambassadors who can help spread the word about your business.

In Chapter Four, we'll dive into the rules and goals for your referral program. Setting clear rules and achievable goals is crucial for success. I'll show you how to establish these and provide examples of effective incentive structures that motivate people to participate.

Chapter Five is all about internal processes and standard operating procedures (SOPs). We'll discuss why it's important to have your internal house in order before launching a referral program. You'll learn how to create and maintain SOPs that keep your business running smoothly and efficiently.

In Chapter Six, we'll look at the importance of documenting processes. Whether you prefer video or text, I'll show you how to create comprehensive guides for your team. Keeping these documents up to date is key, and I'll share tips on how to do that effectively.

Chapter Seven will cover time management and efficiency. We'll explore the value of time studies and how to identify and categorize tasks. I'll teach you how to delegate or outsource tasks that are taking up too much of your time so you can focus on growing your business.

In Chapter Eight, we'll talk about growth and scaling. You'll learn how to balance people, processes, and money to ensure sustainable growth. We'll also cover hiring and training strategies that help you build a strong team.

Chapter Nine will help you build the right team. You'll learn how to identify employees' strengths and place them in roles where they can excel. We'll discuss the importance of building a trusted community of professionals and how to leverage your network for business success.

The main objective of this book is to give you a comprehensive understanding of referral programs and how to implement them effectively. By reading this book, you'll learn how to set up and optimize a referral program, increase your customer base, and grow your business sustainably.

This book is intended for entrepreneurs, business owners, marketers, and anyone looking to harness the power of referrals. Whether you're just starting out or looking to improve an existing program, you'll find valuable insights and practical advice here.

To get the most out of this book, I suggest reading it in sequence, as each chapter builds on the previous one. However, if you're seeking specific information, feel free to jump to the chapter addressing your current needs. Use this book as a guide and reference as you build and refine your referral program.

By the end of this book, you'll have a clear roadmap for creating a referral program that drives growth and success for your business. Let's get started on this journey together.

1

UNDERSTANDING REFERRAL PROGRAMS

Referral programs are a powerful tool for businesses of all sizes. At their core, a referral program is a system that rewards customers or clients for bringing in new business through their recommendations. Imagine you run a business, and one of your satisfied customers tells a friend about your services. If that friend then becomes a new customer, the original customer receives a reward for their referral. It's a simple yet effective concept that leverages the satisfaction and network of your existing clients to generate new business.

The key components of a referral program are straight-forward. First, you have the referrers, who are your current customers or partners willing to promote your business. Next are the incentives, which are the rewards you offer for successful referrals. These can be discounts, cash bonuses, or other perks. Then, there's the tracking system, which ensures that referrals are properly recorded and that rewards are given accurately. Finally, the rewards themselves must be valuable enough to motivate your referrers but sustainable for your business.

The purpose of a referral program is twofold. It aims to attract new customers through trusted recommendations and seeks to strengthen relationships with existing customers by offering them something valuable in return for their loyalty and advocacy. In essence, a good referral program creates a win-win situation for both the business and its customers.

To understand how referral programs evolved, we need to look back at the origins of word-of-mouth marketing. Long before the internet and modern advertising, people relied on the recommendations of friends and family when making purchasing decisions. This informal word-of-mouth was the earliest form of referral marketing. For example, in small-town markets, a recommendation from a neighbor could significantly influence where people choose to shop or which services they use.

As businesses grew and markets expanded, the need for more structured referral systems became apparent. Companies began to recognize the value of formalizing these recommendations to reach a broader audience and track the results. One milestone in the evolution of referral programs was the introduction of customer referral cards and coupons, which provided a tangible way to track referrals and reward customers. Another significant development was the rise of affiliate marketing in the digital age, where businesses created detailed programs to track online referrals and pay commissions to referrers.

A great example of an early successful referral program comes from a well-known online payment platform. They launched a referral program offering cash bonuses to users who referred new members. This program was incredibly effective, helping the company grow its user base exponentially in a short period. The success of this and similar programs highlighted the potential of structured referral systems and inspired many other businesses to adopt similar strategies.

Understanding these foundational elements and the history of referral programs sets the stage for exploring how to create and optimize your own referral program. By tapping into the power of referrals, you can build a strong, loyal customer base and drive sustainable growth for your business.

TYPES OF REFERRAL PROGRAMS

There are several referral programs, each with its unique approach and benefits. Understanding these different types can help you decide which one best suits your business needs.

Direct referral programs are the most straightforward. In a direct referral system, your existing customers or partners refer new clients to your business. For example, if you own a gym and one of your members brings in a friend who signs up for a membership, you might reward the referrer with a discount or a free month. This simple and personal approach leverages your existing customers' trust and relationships. The main benefit of direct referral programs is their simplicity and the strong personal connection they create. However, tracking referrals and ensuring everyone gets their rewards can sometimes be challenging, especially as your business grows.

Affiliate programs take the referral concept to another level by involving a broader network of people who promote your business online. Affiliates are typically bloggers, influencers, or other online content creators who share links to your products or services on their platforms. When someone clicks on an affiliate link and makes a purchase, the affiliate earns a commission. This type of program is particularly effective for online businesses because it can reach a large audience quickly. The key difference between affiliate programs and traditional referral programs is that affiliates may not necessarily be your customers. They are motivated by their commission rather than a personal relationship with your business. This broader reach can be a double-edged sword, as it can bring in a lot of new customers. However, careful management is required to ensure the quality of referrals and prevent fraud.

Influencer and ambassador programs represent a modern twist on the traditional referral model. Influencers are individuals with significant followings on social media platforms who can promote your products to their audience. Brand ambassadors, on the other hand, are loyal customers who represent your brand more formally, often creating content and engaging with potential customers on your behalf. Both influencers and ambassadors help amplify your brand's reach and credibility. For instance, a popular fitness influencer might share their positive experience with your gym, attracting their followers to check it out. The success of these programs often hinges on the authenticity of the endorsements. Audiences can tell when a recommendation is genuine, making influencer and ambassador programs highly effective. However, finding the right influencers and managing these relationships can be resource intensive.

Each type of referral program has advantages and challenges. Direct referral programs build on personal trust, affiliate programs leverage online reach, and influencer programs tap into the credibility of well-known personalities. By understanding these different models, you can choose the best approach for your business and maximize the benefits of referral marketing.

Key Components of a Referral Program

When you set up a referral program, there are several key components you need to consider. Let's break them down.

First, think about the referrers. These are the people who will be spreading the word about your business. They could be your customers, employees, or business partners. Each group has its own strengths. Customers' firsthand experience with your product or service makes their recommendations credible. Employees are deeply familiar with your business and can provide detailed insights. Partners can reach new audiences you might not have access to on your own. To identify potential referrers, look for those who are already enthusiastic about your business. Engage with them regularly, show your appreciation, and make them feel valued. This can be done through personal interactions, special events, or recognition programs.

Next, let's talk about incentives. People need a reason to refer others to your business. The incentives you offer can vary. Monetary rewards are straightforward and often effective. Discounts on future purchases can also be a good motivator, especially for customers who already love your products. Exclusive access to new products or special events can appeal to those who value unique experiences. The key is to design attractive yet sustainable incentives for your business. It's important to be clear and transparent about what referrers will get and when. The rewards should be fair and proportional to the effort and value of the referral.

Tracking systems are crucial for the success of your referral program. You must accurately track who is referring whom and ensure everyone gets their rewards. There are several methods and tools for tracking referrals. Some businesses use simple spreadsheets, while others invest in specialized referral software. Whatever method you choose, it's important to maintain transparency and build trust with your referrers. They should be able to see the status of their referrals and know when they can expect their rewards. This transparency builds trust and encourages more referrals, as people feel confident that their efforts will be recognized.

By focusing on these key components—referrers, incentives, and tracking systems—you can create an effective and sustainable referral program. Your referrers will feel motivated and appreciated, and your business will benefit from a steady stream of new customers brought in through trusted recommendations. This approach ensures that everyone involved wins, which is the goal of any referral program.

Benefits of Referral Programs

Referral programs are incredibly beneficial for businesses, especially when it comes to acquiring new customers. Unlike traditional advertising methods, which often require significant upfront investment and can be hit or miss in terms of effectiveness, referral programs leverage the trust and satisfaction of your existing customers. When a customer refers someone to your business, that new potential customer is coming in with a built-in recommendation. This makes them more likely to trust your business and become paying customers. The power of personal recommendation is immense. People trust the opinions of their friends and family more than any advertisement they might see on TV or online.

Comparing referral programs to other customer acquisition methods, the differences are striking. Traditional advertising methods, like TV commercials or online ads, often cast a wide net in hopes of catching a few interested customers. This can be expensive and inefficient. Referral programs, on the other hand, are targeted and personal. They bring in customers who are already somewhat pre-qualified because they come through a trusted source. This makes the acquisition process smoother and more cost-effective.

Referral programs also play a crucial role in increasing customer loyalty. When customers are encouraged to refer others, they become more invested in your business. They feel a sense of ownership and pride in helping your business grow. This deepens their connection to your brand. For example, a popular coffee shop might offer a free drink for every friend a customer refers. This brings in new customers and encourages the referring customer to return more frequently to enjoy their rewards. It's a win-win situation that strengthens the relationship between your business and its customers.

Moreover, loyal customers who participate in referral programs are likely to spread positive word-of-mouth even beyond the scope of the program. They become brand advocates who talk about your business in everyday conversations, online reviews, and social media posts. This organic promotion is incredibly valuable and hard to replicate with paid advertising.

When it comes to cost-effectiveness, referral programs shine. The initial setup might require some investment in creating the program and promoting it to your customers, but the ongoing costs are typically low. You're paying for results—new customers—rather than upfront costs with no guarantee of return. Let's look at a case study. A software company decided to implement a referral program, offering their users a free month of service for every new customer they brought in. The program quickly paid for itself as the cost of offering a free month was significantly lower than the cost of acquiring a new customer through paid advertising. Plus, the new customers brought in through referrals tended to be more loyal and stayed longer than those acquired through other methods. This created a snowball effect, where the initial investment led to ongoing growth and profitability.

In conclusion, referral programs are powerful for customer acquisition, fostering loyalty, and managing costs. By leveraging the trust and satisfaction of your existing customers, you can attract new customers more efficiently and effectively. The benefits of referral programs are clear, and when done right, they can be a game-changer for your business.

STATISTICS AND DATA

Statistics and data are vital when it comes to understanding the effectiveness of referral programs. Numbers tell the story of how powerful these programs can be. For example, data shows that customers acquired through referrals have a 37 percent higher retention rate compared to those acquired through other means. This means that referred customers tend to stick around longer, becoming loyal patrons who continue to bring value to your business over time.

In different industries, the impact of referral programs varies but consistently shows positive results. In the tech industry, referral programs can account for up to 50 percent of new customer acquisitions. In retail, referral programs can increase sales by 20 to 30 percent. These numbers highlight that businesses are seeing significant benefits from implementing referral programs across various sectors.

When we look at the return on investment (ROI) for referral programs, the data is compelling. Referral programs often cost less per acquisition than traditional marketing strategies. For instance, a study found that the cost of acquiring a customer through referrals is $23, whereas the cost through paid advertising can be upwards of $100. This significant difference in cost underscores the efficiency of referral programs.

Let's consider some examples. A popular ride-sharing company launched a referral program offering free rides to both the referrer and the new customer. This program brought in millions of new users and created a network effect where existing users were highly motivated to bring in more users. The ROI from this program was substantial, far exceeding that of their other marketing efforts.

Another example comes from an online payment platform that saw its user base grow exponentially through a referral program that offered cash bonuses. This program proved to be a cost-effective way to acquire new users, as the cost of the bonus was much lower than what they would have spent on traditional advertising for the same number of new users. The long-term value of these referred customers also turned out to be higher, adding even more to the program's success.

These examples illustrate that referral programs not only bring in new customers but do so in a cost-effective and sustainable way. The data supports the conclusion that referral programs can be a highly effective part of your marketing strategy. By focusing on the quality of customer relationships and leveraging the trust between your existing customers and their networks, you can achieve impressive growth and a high return on your investment. This makes referral programs a smart choice for any business looking to expand its customer base efficiently.

Common Challenges and Solutions

Starting a referral program can feel daunting, and facing some challenges along the way is normal. One of the first hurdles is overcoming initial hesitation. Many business owners worry that their customers might not be interested in participating or that the program will be too complicated to manage. These concerns are valid but can be addressed with straightforward strategies.

One common misconception is that customers won't want to refer others without significant incentives. While incentives are important, many customers are happy to recommend a business they believe in, especially if they have had a great experience. The key is communicating the benefits clearly and making the process as simple as possible. Start by asking your most loyal customers for referrals and offering them an attractive incentive to kickstart the program. Personalizing your request can also make a big difference. Customers are more likely to participate when they feel appreciated and see the value in what they are sharing.

The next challenge is maintaining engagement once the program is up and running. Keeping your referrers motivated over the long term requires ongoing effort. Regular communication is essential. Send out updates about the program, highlight success stories, and remind customers of the rewards they can earn. It's also important to periodically review and update the program. This can mean adjusting incentives based on what's working, adding new features to keep things fresh, or addressing any feedback from participants. By showing that the program is active and evolving, you keep it at the top of your referrers' minds.

Accurate tracking and fair reward distribution are crucial for the program's credibility. If customers feel that their referrals are not being properly tracked or that rewards are not distributed fairly, they will lose trust in the program. Using reliable tracking tools is essential. Whether it's software specifically designed for referral programs or a well-organized manual system, ensure that every referral is recorded accurately. Transparency is also key. Allow your referrers to track their progress and see the status of their referrals.

Reward distribution can also be challenging but manageable with the right approach. Set clear guidelines for when and how rewards are given out. Communicate these guidelines clearly to your referrers so they know what to expect. Timely distribution of rewards is crucial. The quicker you can reward your referrers, the more motivated they will be to continue participating. If any issues arise, address them promptly and fairly to maintain trust.

By anticipating these common challenges and having strategies to address them, you can create a referral program that is effective and sustainable. The effort you put into overcoming initial hesitation, maintaining engagement, and ensuring fair tracking and reward distribution will pay off in the form of a robust, trusted program that continuously brings in new customers and fosters loyalty among your existing ones.

SUMMARY AND KEY TAKEAWAYS

As we wrap up this chapter, let's recap the main concepts we've covered about referral programs. We've explored what referral programs are, their key components, and the different types of programs you can implement. We've looked at the benefits, such as customer acquisition, loyalty, and cost-effectiveness, supported by data and examples from various industries. We also addressed common challenges and provided solutions for overcoming them.

To start planning your referral program, consider these practical steps. First, identify potential referrers among your customers, employees, and partners. Engage them with compelling, attractive, and sustainable incentives for your business. Ensure you have a robust tracking system in place to accurately record referrals and manage rewards. Regularly update and communicate with your referrers to keep them motivated and engaged.

The next chapter will dive into the triangle principle. This principle is all about creating a win-win-win scenario, ensuring every referral benefits not just you and the referrer but also the new customer. We'll explore how this approach can guide your business decisions and help you build a referral program that's even more effective and sustainable.

By understanding these key points and taking action, you'll be well on your way to creating a referral program that drives growth and builds strong customer relationships. Let's move forward with the confidence that you can harness the power of referrals to take your business to new heights.

2

THE TRIANGLE PRINCIPLE

The triangle principle is a powerful concept that I rely on in business, especially when it comes to referral programs. Imagine a triangle where each corner represents a key player: the business, the referrer, and the new customer. This simple shape illustrates the interconnectedness and balance needed for a referral program to thrive.

The business sits at one corner of the triangle. It provides the products or services and sets up the referral program. At the second corner, the referrer is a satisfied customer or partner who recommends the business to others. The new customer, who takes a recommendation and decides to try the business, occupies the third corner. The strength of this triangle lies in its balance. Each party must benefit from the arrangement for it to be successful.

Creating win-win-win scenarios is essential for long-term success. When all three parties benefit, the system is self-sustaining. The business gains new customers, increasing revenue and growth. The referrer feels appreciated and valued, often receiving rewards or recognition for their efforts. The new customer benefits from a trusted recommendation, which often leads to a better purchasing experience.

This approach leads to high customer satisfaction. People are more likely to trust and be satisfied with a service recommended by someone they know. This trust translates into loyalty. Customers who come through referrals tend to stay longer and engage more with the business. They are not just one-time buyers but potential lifelong customers.

Loyal customers, in turn, are likely to become referrers themselves, creating a positive feedback loop. As the program grows, the business sees a steady stream of new customers brought in by satisfied existing ones. This boosts sales and reduces marketing costs, as word-of-mouth referrals are far cheaper than traditional advertising.

The benefits of the triangle principle extend beyond individual transactions. It fosters a community around the business, where customers feel like they are part of something bigger. This sense of belonging can be a powerful driver of growth and engagement. People like to support businesses they feel connected to, and referral programs based on the triangle principle strengthen these connections.

The triangle principle shows how interconnected and mutually beneficial relationships drive successful referral programs. By creating win-win-win scenarios, businesses can ensure that their referral programs are effective and sustainable, leading to long-term growth and customer loyalty.

The Three Points of the Triangle

The triangle principle relies on the interconnectedness of three crucial points: the business, the referrer, and the new customer. Each point plays a vital role in the success of a referral program.

First, let's talk about the business. The business is at the heart of the referral program, providing the products or services that are being recommended. It's the business's responsibility to create an attractive and rewarding referral program. The business must offer compelling incentives that motivate participation to provide value to both the referrer and the new customer. This could be discounts, exclusive access to new products, or monetary rewards. Additionally, the business must ensure that the referral process is seamless and easy to navigate. A well-implemented referral program can significantly benefit the business by increasing customer acquisition, enhancing customer loyalty, and reducing marketing costs. For example, a software company that offers a month of free service for each successful referral attracts new users and strengthens its relationship with existing customers.

Now, let's focus on the referrer. The referrer is often a satisfied customer or a partner who believes in the business and is willing to recommend it to others. The role of the referrer is crucial because their endorsement carries weight and trust. Engaging and motivating referrers requires thoughtful strategies. Regular communication, personalized rewards, and public recognition are effective ways to keep referrers engaged. For instance, a beauty salon might send personalized thank-you notes and offer free treatments for each referral, making referrers feel valued and appreciated. By feeling recognized and rewarded, referrers are more likely to continue recommending the business to others, creating a steady flow of new customers.

Finally, we come to the new customer. The new customer fits into the triangle as the recipient of the referral. Ensuring that their first experience with the business is positive is essential. A new customer who is referred to your business comes with a level of trust and expectation set by the referrer. Meeting or exceeding these expectations is key to turning them into loyal clients. This can be achieved through excellent customer service, personalized onboarding experiences, and follow-up communications. For example, a fitness club might offer a free introductory session and a personalized fitness plan to new members referred by existing clients. This not only makes the new customer feel welcomed but also sets a positive tone for their ongoing relationship with the business.

Each point of the triangle—the business, the referrer, and the new customer—is interconnected and relies on the others for success. The business must create value, the referrer must feel motivated and appreciated, and the new customer must have a positive experience. Businesses can create a powerful referral program that drives growth and builds strong, lasting relationships by focusing on these three points and ensuring that each one benefits.

IMPLEMENTING THE TRIANGLE PRINCIPLE

Implementing the triangle principle is about creating a win-win-win scenario where the business, the referrer, and the new customer all benefit. This approach ensures the program is sustainable and mutually rewarding for everyone involved.

To begin, we need a step-by-step guide to designing a referral program grounded in the triangle principle. The first step is to define clear goals for each party. For the business, the primary goal is often to acquire new customers and increase revenue. The goal for the referrer is to feel appreciated and rewarded for their efforts. For the new customer, the goal is to have a positive and satisfying first experience with the business.

Once these goals are identified, the next step is to align them. Start by considering what motivates your referrers. If they are existing customers, think about what rewards would encourage them to refer others. This might be discounts, exclusive offers, or even public recognition. For example, a local coffee shop might offer a free drink for every new customer a referrer brings in. This reward is simple but effective, providing immediate gratification to the referrer.

For the new customer, the key is to make their introduction to your business as smooth and rewarding as possible. This means providing an exceptional first experience that meets or exceeds their expectations. Suppose a new customer is referred to a fitness club. In that case, the club could offer a complimentary training session and a personalized fitness plan. This approach makes the new customer feel valued and increases the likelihood they will become a loyal member.

With the goals aligned, the next step is to set up a tracking system to ensure that referrals are accurately recorded and rewarded. This might involve using software to automate the process or manually tracking referrals through a well-organized system. The important thing is to ensure transparency and reliability so that referrers trust that their efforts will be rewarded fairly.

The final step is regularly reviewing and adjusting the program to keep it effective and engaging. This involves gathering feedback from referrers and new customers to understand what's working and what could be improved. Regular updates and enhancements to the program can keep it fresh and exciting, encouraging ongoing participation.

Creating a win-win-win scenario through the triangle principle is about more than just setting up a referral program. It's about fostering a community where the business, referrers, and new customers all feel connected and valued. By aligning the goals of each party and ensuring that everyone benefits, you can build a referral program that drives growth and strengthens relationships and loyalty across the board.

Benefits of the Triangle Principle

The triangle principle offers numerous benefits, transforming how businesses engage with their customers and referrers. One of the most significant advantages is enhanced customer loyalty.

By focusing on creating win-win-win scenarios, businesses can foster stronger relationships with their customers and referrers. When customers feel valued and rewarded for their referrals, they are more likely to stay loyal to the business. This loyalty is reflected in repeat business and long-term relationships.

Data supports this. For instance, a study showed that customers who come through referrals have a 37 percent higher retention rate compared to those acquired through other means. This is because referred customers often start with a higher level of trust and satisfaction, as they come recommended by someone they know and trust. This higher retention rate translates into more repeat business and a steady stream of revenue.

Another benefit of the triangle principle is increased referrals. A successful referral program creates a positive feedback loop. As customers experience the benefits of the referral program, they are more likely to refer others, knowing they will be rewarded. This leads to more frequent and higher-quality referrals. For example, a restaurant offering a free meal for every new customer referred might significantly increase referrals, as satisfied customers eagerly share their positive experiences with friends and family.

The long-term benefits of creating a balanced and mutually beneficial referral ecosystem are evident in sustainable business growth. When a business consistently provides value to referrers and new customers, it builds a strong, loyal customer base. This base becomes a foundation for ongoing growth as satisfied customers continue to refer new clients. An excellent example is a tech company that implemented a referral program offering both the referrer and the new customer a discount on their services. Over time, this program not only brought in a substantial number of new clients but also strengthened the loyalty of existing ones, leading to sustained growth.

By leveraging the triangle principle, businesses can create a referral program that attracts new customers and strengthens relationships with existing ones. This approach ensures that everyone involved benefits, leading to a more robust and sustainable business. The data and examples highlight the effectiveness of this principle, demonstrating how it can drive long-term success and growth.

CHALLENGES AND SOLUTIONS

Implementing the triangle principle in your referral program can present several challenges. Understanding these potential obstacles and knowing how to address them is crucial for success.

One common challenge is the misalignment of goals. The business, the referrer, and the new customer all have different expectations; if these are not aligned, the program can fail. For instance, the business might focus solely on acquiring new customers without considering the needs of the referrer or the new customer. This can lead to dissatisfaction and a lack of participation. Inadequate incentives can also be a stumbling block. If the rewards for referring new customers are not attractive enough, referrers may not be motivated to participate. Similarly, if the new customers do not see value in being referred, they might not follow through. Poor tracking systems pose another significant issue. Without accurate tracking, referrals can get lost, and referrers may not receive their due rewards, leading to frustration and disengagement.

To overcome these challenges, start by clearly defining and aligning the goals of all parties involved. Ensure that the benefits for the business, the referrer, and the new customer are well-balanced and communicated effectively. This alignment can be achieved through regular feedback and adjustments based on the needs and expectations of each group.

For example, if you notice that referrers are not engaging with the program, consider enhancing the incentives. Offering tiered rewards or exclusive benefits can increase motivation. Similarly, if new customers are not converting, look at ways to improve their onboarding experience to make it more appealing and seamless.

Improving tracking systems is also essential. Invest in reliable referral-tracking software that provides transparency and ensures accuracy. This allows referrers to track their progress and trust that they will be rewarded fairly. If manual tracking is used, ensure it is meticulously organized and regularly updated to prevent oversights.

Adjustments and improvements are part of the process. Regularly review the referral program's performance and gather feedback from participants. For instance, a fitness center might notice that its referral program incentives are not attracting enough new members. By surveying their referrers, they might discover that offering free personal training sessions, rather than just discounts, would be more appealing. Implementing this change can re-energize the program and align it better with what participants value.

By addressing these challenges with practical solutions, you can maintain a balanced and effective referral program based on the triangle principle. It's about balancing the business's goals, the referrer's motivations, and the new customer's expectations. With careful planning and regular adjustments, you can ensure that your referral program runs smoothly and drives significant growth for your business.

MEASURING SUCCESS

Measuring the success of your referral program is crucial to understanding its impact and making necessary adjustments.

Key metrics help you gauge how well the triangle principle is working and where improvements can be made.

To start, track the number of new customers acquired through referrals. This metric shows the direct impact of your program on customer acquisition. Compare this number to other acquisition channels to see how effective your referral program is in bringing in new business. Another important metric is the referral rate, which is the percentage of your existing customers who are referring new ones. A high referral rate indicates that your customers are engaged and motivated by the program.

Customer lifetime value (CLV) is also a key metric. This measures a customer's total revenue over their entire relationship with your business. Referred customers often have a higher CLV because they come in with a positive impression and are more likely to be loyal. Tracking the CLV of referred customers versus non-referred ones can provide insights into the long-term benefits of your referral program.

Your referrers' engagement rates are equally important. Monitor how often referrers participate and how many referrals they generate. This helps identify your most active and valuable referrers, allowing you to nurture these relationships further. It's also useful to track the conversion rate of referrals. This measures how many referred leads turn into paying customers. A high conversion rate suggests that your referrers are bringing in quality leads who are ready to do business with you.

Regularly reviewing and refining your referral program is essential for continuous improvement. Gather feedback from participants to understand their experiences and identify areas for enhancement. Surveys, interviews, and direct feedback can provide valuable insights. For example, referrers might feel the incentive structure is not compelling enough or that new customers would appreciate a more streamlined onboarding process.

Use data to make informed decisions. Analyzing the metrics and feedback helps you spot trends and areas for improvement. For instance, if you notice a drop in engagement, you might need to adjust your communication strategy or introduce new incentives. If the conversion rate is lower than expected, evaluate the quality of the leads being referred and consider ways to better qualify them.

Implementing changes based on data and feedback keeps your referral program dynamic and responsive to the needs of your participants. It also ensures that the program remains effective in driving growth and maintaining strong relationships with both referrers and new customers.

By consistently measuring success and striving for continuous improvement, you can maintain a referral program that not only brings in new business but also enhances customer loyalty and satisfaction. This proactive approach helps ensure that your referral program remains a powerful tool for growth and engagement.

Summary and Key Takeaways

In this chapter, we've covered a lot of ground about the triangle principle and its role in creating a successful referral program. To recap, the triangle principle is about ensuring that the business, the referrer, and the new customer all benefit from the referral process. This win-win-win scenario builds a solid foundation for long-term success. By focusing on these three interconnected points, businesses can create a balanced and effective referral program that drives growth, enhances customer loyalty, and brings in high-quality referrals.

Here are some practical steps to start implementing the triangle principle in your referral program. Begin by clearly defining the goals for each party involved. Make sure that the incentives for referrers are attractive and that the onboarding process for new customers is seamless and welcoming. Invest in a robust tracking system to ensure that all referrals are accurately recorded and rewards are fairly distributed. Regularly review and adjust the program based on feedback and performance data to keep it effective and engaging.

The next chapter will delve into the nuts and bolts of setting up your referral program from scratch. We'll explore how to engage your community of referrers, create compelling incentives, and ensure a smooth and rewarding experience for new customers. By following the guidelines laid out in this chapter, you'll be well-prepared to build a referral program that not only meets but exceeds your business goals. Stay tuned for actionable strategies and insights that will help you take your referral program to the next level.

3

SETTING UP YOUR REFERRAL PROGRAM

Setting up a referral program can be one of the most rewarding strategies for any business. A well-structured referral program brings in new customers and strengthens relationships with your existing clients. When done correctly, it becomes a powerful tool for sustainable growth.

A well-designed referral program offers numerous benefits. It harnesses the power of word-of-mouth marketing, which is often more trusted and effective than traditional advertising. People tend to trust recommendations from friends and family over ads. By leveraging this trust, you can attract high-quality leads who are more likely to become loyal customers.

Additionally, referral programs can significantly reduce customer acquisition costs. Instead of spending large sums on advertising, you can incentivize your current customers to bring in new business. This saves money and creates a more engaged and loyal customer base. Customers who participate in referral programs often feel more connected to the business and are more likely to continue using your products or services.

Setting up your referral program correctly from the start is crucial for long-term success. It's not just about offering rewards; it's about creating a seamless and motivating system that works for everyone involved. By planning and implementing each aspect thoughtfully, you can ensure that your program runs smoothly and effectively.

INITIAL STEPS

The first steps in setting up your referral program are identifying potential referrers and defining your goals. You need to understand who will most effectively bring in new customers. These could be your existing customers, employees, or business partners. Each group has its own strengths and can bring unique value to your program.

Once you've identified your potential referrers, engaging them from the start is important. Communicate clearly about the program, the rewards they can earn, and how they can participate. Make sure they understand how easy it is to refer others and how beneficial it can be for them.

Defining your goals is the next crucial step. What do you want to achieve with your referral program? Are you looking to increase sales, grow your customer base, or enhance customer loyalty? Setting clear, measurable goals will help you design a program that aligns with your overall business objectives and allows you to track its success.

As you move forward, remember that the foundation you lay in these initial steps will set the tone for the entire program. By carefully planning and engaging the right people, you'll be well on your way to creating a referral program that drives growth and builds lasting relationships.

DESIGNING ATTRACTIVE INCENTIVES

Creating the right incentives is crucial for the success of your referral program. The type of incentive you choose can make or break the program. There are several options to consider, each with its own advantages and disadvantages.

Monetary rewards are straightforward and often very appealing. Offering cash incentives or gift cards can quickly attract participants because everyone appreciates tangible rewards. However, the downside is that monetary rewards can become expensive for the business, especially if the program scales up quickly.

Discounts on future purchases are another popular choice. They provide value to both the referrer and the new customer, encouraging repeat business. This type of incentive can foster loyalty and increase the lifetime value of your customers. The challenge here is to ensure that the discounts are attractive enough to motivate referrals without cutting too deeply into your profit margins.

Exclusive access is a unique approach. This could be early access to new products, special events, or VIP treatment. These incentives can create a sense of exclusivity and appreciation among your referrers. The main drawback is that these types of rewards might not appeal to everyone, and their effectiveness can vary depending on your audience.

When designing your reward structure, consider creating a tiered system. A tiered reward system offers increasing incentives based on the number of referrals made. For example, the first referral might earn a small discount, the second a larger one, and so on, culminating in a significant reward for a high number of referrals. This motivates referrers to keep participating and builds excitement and a sense of progression.

Balancing the attractiveness of rewards with cost-effectiveness is essential. You want your incentives to be enticing enough to encourage participation but sustainable for your business in the long run. Analyzing the cost per acquisition and the expected lifetime value of referred customers can help you find the right balance.

Distributing incentives fairly and promptly is another key factor. Best practices for distribution include setting clear guidelines on when and how rewards will be given. For instance, rewards could be issued once the new customer makes their first purchase or after a specific period of sustained engagement. Ensuring transparency in the reward distribution process builds trust and encourages ongoing participation. Referrers should always be able to see the status of their referrals and understand when they can expect their rewards.

Developing a Tracking System

A reliable tracking system is the backbone of any successful referral program. The right tools can streamline the process, ensuring that every referral is accurately recorded and rewarded.

Choosing the right tracking tools is the first step. Numerous software options are available, each with its own set of features. Some programs are simple and easy to use, while others offer more advanced capabilities like automated reward distribution, detailed analytics, and integration with other business systems. When selecting a tool, consider your business size, specific needs, and budget. Look for software that offers a balance between functionality and ease of use.

Once you've chosen your tracking tool, the next step is implementation. This involves setting up the system to accurately capture referral data and ensure it integrates smoothly with your existing processes. A step-by-step guide can help here: start by configuring the software to match your referral program's structure, test it thoroughly to iron out any kinks, and then train your team to use it effectively.

Accuracy and reliability in tracking are paramount. Any errors in recording referrals can lead to frustration and a loss of trust among your participants. Regular audits of the system can help catch and correct any issues early on.

Maintaining transparency throughout the referral process is crucial for building trust. Allowing referrers to track their own progress is a great way to achieve this. Provide them with access to a dashboard where they can see the status of their referrals, the rewards they've earned, and any pending rewards. Transparency builds trust and motivates referrers to keep participating as they can clearly see the benefits of their efforts.

By carefully designing your incentive structure and implementing a robust tracking system, you can create an attractive and effective referral program. This approach ensures that all participants feel valued and that the program runs smoothly, driving growth and fostering loyalty for your business.

CREATING MARKETING MATERIALS

Crafting the message for your referral program is crucial. You need to clearly communicate the benefits to potential referrers in a way that grabs their attention and makes them want to participate. Start by highlighting what's in it for them. People are more likely to engage if they understand how they will benefit. Whether it's cash rewards, discounts, or exclusive access, make sure your message conveys the value of participating in your referral program.

For example, a simple and effective message could be: "Refer a friend and get $50 off your next purchase! Help your friends discover our amazing products and earn rewards for yourself." This message is straightforward, easy to understand, and highlights both the action required (referring a friend) and the reward (a $50 discount).

Designing promotional materials is another important step. Your brochures, emails, and social media posts should be attractive and informative. Use eye-catching graphics and clear, concise text. The goal is to capture attention quickly and convey the essential information without overwhelming the reader. High-quality visuals and a clean, professional design can make a big difference.

For brochures and emails, include testimonials from satisfied customers who have benefited from your referral program. Real-life examples add credibility and make the program more relatable. Use engaging images or short videos on social media to explain how the program works and what participants can gain.

Leveraging digital platforms is key to spreading the word about your referral program. Your website should have a dedicated page explaining the program in detail, with easy-to-find links for signing up. Social media is a powerful tool for reaching a broad audience quickly. Regular posts about the program, along with updates and success stories, can keep it at the top of your followers' minds.

Email marketing is another effective channel. Send out regular newsletters highlighting the referral program and any new developments or incentives. Integrating referral program promotions into your existing marketing efforts ensures a consistent message across all platforms. This integrated approach helps build awareness and drives participation.

Launching Your Referral Program

Before launching your referral program, ensuring everything is in place is essential. Go through a final checklist to make sure you haven't missed any critical steps. Test the system thoroughly to ensure it works smoothly. This includes ensuring that referrals are tracked accurately and rewards are distributed correctly. Conduct a few test runs with trusted customers or employees to iron out any kinks.

When you're ready to launch, having a clear strategy can make all the difference. Start by engaging your initial referrers—these could be your most loyal customers or employees.

Give them a sneak peek of the program and maybe even a special incentive for being among the first to participate. Their enthusiasm can help generate early momentum.

Use a mix of online and offline tactics to announce the launch. Send out email blasts, post on social media, and use in-store signage if applicable. Make a big deal out of the launch to create excitement and encourage people to join in.

Collecting and analyzing feedback from early participants is crucial. Pay attention to what's working and what isn't. Are there any common questions or issues that keep coming up? Use this feedback to make necessary adjustments. Maybe you need to tweak the incentive structure or clarify the referral process. Being responsive and making improvements based on real feedback will help ensure the program's long-term success.

By carefully crafting your marketing materials, leveraging digital platforms, and executing a well-planned launch strategy, you can set your referral program up for success. Remember, the goal is to create a seamless, rewarding experience that motivates people to refer others and keeps them coming back. With thoughtful planning and execution, your referral program can become a powerful tool for growing your business.

Engaging and Motivating Referrers

Engaging and motivating your referrers is crucial to the success of your referral program. Ongoing communication is key to keeping them informed and enthusiastic. Regular updates are essential. Let your referrers know how the program is going, share success stories, and remind them of the rewards they can earn. This keeps the program fresh in their minds and encourages continued participation.

One effective strategy for maintaining enthusiasm is to create a sense of anticipation and excitement around your updates. Maybe you launch a new incentive or highlight a particularly successful referrer. Keeping things dynamic and engaging helps to sustain interest. For example, a quarterly newsletter featuring top referrers and new rewards can go a long way in maintaining engagement.

Recognizing and rewarding your top referrers is another powerful tool. People love being acknowledged for their efforts. Highlighting the most active referrers in your communications makes them feel appreciated and inspires others to step up their game. Consider creating a leaderboard or a reward system that recognizes the top performers. This creates a friendly sense of competition and fosters a community of engaged participants.

To support your referrers, provide them with the tools and resources they need to succeed. This could include marketing materials, referral templates, or even training sessions on how to effectively refer new customers. Promptly addressing any questions or concerns is also vital. A responsive support system ensures that your referrers feel valued and supported, which can significantly boost their motivation.

Measuring and Analyzing Performance

To ensure your referral program is effective, you need to measure and analyze its performance regularly. Key metrics provide valuable insights into how well the program is working and where improvements can be made. Track metrics such as the number of new customers acquired through referrals, the referral rate, and the conversion rate of referrals. These numbers help you understand the program's direct impact on your customer base.

Interpreting these metrics allows you to make informed, data-driven decisions. For instance, if you notice a high referral rate but a low conversion rate, it might indicate that while people are referring, the new leads are not following through.

This could mean you need to improve your onboarding process for new customers.

Regular reviews and reports are essential for keeping track of your progress. Set up a schedule for these reviews—monthly, quarterly, or whatever fits best with your business rhythms. Detailed reports should provide a clear picture of the program's performance, highlighting successes and areas needing attention. These reports serve as a roadmap for future improvements.

Continuous improvement is the goal. Use the feedback from your referrers and the performance data to refine and enhance the referral program. If you see that certain incentives are not working as well as others, don't hesitate to adjust them. Keep the program fresh and effective by regularly introducing new elements and responding to the needs and preferences of your referrers.

Strategies for keeping the program effective over time include rotating rewards to keep things interesting, introducing special promotions, and ensuring that communication remains engaging and relevant. By staying proactive and responsive, you can maintain a vibrant referral program that continues to drive growth and foster loyalty.

In conclusion, by maintaining ongoing communication, recognizing and rewarding your top referrers, providing the necessary support, and continuously measuring and improving your program, you can create a referral system that attracts new customers and keeps your existing ones engaged and motivated. This balanced approach ensures long-term success and sustainable growth for your business.

Summary and Key Takeaways

This chapter explored the essentials of setting up a referral program and the importance of doing it right from the start. We began by discussing the benefits of a well-structured referral

program, emphasizing how it can drive new customer acquisition, enhance customer loyalty, and reduce marketing costs.
These advantages stem from leveraging the trust and satisfaction of your existing customers to bring in high-quality leads.

We then moved on to the initial steps of identifying
potential referrers and defining clear goals for your program.
Knowing who your referrers are and what motivates them is
crucial. Equally important is setting measurable objectives
that align with your overall business strategy.

Next, we covered the design of attractive incentives. We
examined different types of rewards, from monetary incentives
to exclusive access, and discussed how to create a reward structure that motivates participation while remaining cost-effective.
We also highlighted the importance of distributing these
rewards fairly and transparently to build trust and encourage
ongoing engagement.

Developing a robust tracking system is another critical
element. We talked about choosing the right tools and implementing a system that ensures accurate and reliable tracking
of referrals. Transparency is key here, as it allows referrers to
see their progress and builds confidence in the program.

Creating compelling marketing materials and leveraging
digital platforms were also discussed. Effective communication
and engaging promotional materials are essential for spreading
the word about your referral program and attracting participants. Integrating these efforts into your existing marketing
strategy ensures a consistent message across all channels.

Finally, we addressed the importance of ongoing
engagement and motivation for your referrers. Regular communication, recognizing top performers, and providing support
are all strategies that keep referrers active and enthusiastic.
Measuring and analyzing performance through key metrics helps you understand the program's impact and make
data-driven improvements.

As you begin setting up your referral program, here are some practical steps to take. Start by identifying and engaging your potential referrers with clear communication and attractive incentives. Implement a reliable tracking system to ensure transparency and accuracy. Create compelling marketing materials and promote the program across all your digital platforms. Keep your referrers engaged with regular updates, recognition, and support. Finally, continuously measure performance and make adjustments based on feedback and data to keep the program effective and motivating.

Looking ahead to the next chapter, we'll dive deeper into engaging your community of referrers and maintaining momentum in your referral program. We'll explore strategies for keeping the program dynamic and fresh, ensuring sustained participation and long-term success. Stay tuned for more insights and practical advice on building a thriving referral ecosystem.

4

RULES AND GOALS

Setting up a referral program can be a game-changer for your business, but its success largely depends on the foundation you lay from the start. Clear rules and goals are the bedrock of a robust referral program. Without them, you risk confusion, frustration, and, ultimately, a failed initiative.

Establishing clear rules is crucial because it sets the boundaries and expectations for everyone involved. Your customers need to understand exactly what qualifies as a referral, how they can participate, and what rewards they can earn. Clear rules eliminate ambiguity and ensure that all participants are on the same page. This clarity helps in building trust, as participants know the program is fair and transparent.

On the other hand, setting well-defined goals gives your referral program direction and purpose. Goals help you measure success and identify areas for improvement. They align your referral efforts with your overall business objectives, ensuring that the program contributes meaningfully to your growth strategy. For instance, if one of your business objectives is to expand your customer base, your referral program goals might focus on the number of new customers acquired through referrals.

Clear rules and goals not only provide structure but also enhance the sustainability of your referral program. When participants understand the rules and see clear goals, they are more likely to stay engaged over the long term. This engagement is vital for maintaining momentum and ensuring continuous growth.

In summary, the importance of clear rules and goals in a referral program cannot be overstated. They lay the groundwork for a program that is fair, transparent, and aligned with your business objectives. With a strong foundation, your referral program can thrive, driving sustainable growth and long-term success.

ESTABLISHING CLEAR RULES

When creating a referral program, the first step is to define eligibility. You need to be specific about who can participate. Your customers are the obvious choice, but consider including employees and business partners as well. Each group brings different strengths to the table. For example, customers can provide personal testimonials, while employees might have insider knowledge that adds credibility. However, it's important to set some restrictions. Geographic limitations might be necessary if your business only operates in certain areas. Additionally, there might be certain business relationships that could complicate referrals, such as vendors or contractors, who should be excluded to avoid conflicts of interest.

Once you've defined who can participate, the next step is to establish clear referral process guidelines. This means providing a step-by-step explanation of how the referral process works. For instance, if a customer wants to refer a friend, what are the exact steps they need to take? Should they fill out a form on your website, or is there a special link they need to use? Make sure these instructions are simple and easy to follow. It's also crucial to give detailed instructions to the new referred customers. They need to understand what they need to do to qualify as a successful referral, such as make a purchase or sign up for a service.

Reward conditions are another essential aspect of clear rules. Be explicit about the specific conditions under which rewards are given. Will the referrer receive their reward immediately after the referral makes a purchase, or is there a waiting period? Clearly define what constitutes a successful referral. This clarity not only motivates participants but also prevents misunderstandings and disputes.

Speaking of disputes, it's inevitable that issues will arise from time to time. Therefore, you should have procedures in place for handling any disputes or issues that come up. Clearly outline the steps participants should take if they encounter a problem. Provide contact points and support channels, such as a dedicated email address or a customer service hotline, to ensure they can get help when needed. This proactive approach helps maintain trust and keeps your program running smoothly.

SETTING ACHIEVABLE GOALS

Setting achievable goals for your referral program is crucial for its success. These goals should align with your broader business objectives. For example, if your primary business objective is to increase sales, your referral program goals might focus on the number of new customers acquired through referrals. If you're looking to expand your customer base, you might set targets for the geographic spread of your referrals.

Defining success metrics is the next step. You need to identify key metrics for measuring the success of your referral program. These might include the number of referrals, conversion rates, and customer retention. Setting realistic and achievable targets for each metric is essential. For instance, you might aim to get 50 new referrals in the first month and increase that number gradually over the next few months.

It's important to set both short-term and long-term goals. Short-term goals help you achieve quick wins and build momentum. For example, you might set a goal to reach a certain number of referrals within the first quarter. Long-term goals, on the other hand, provide direction and focus for sustained growth. You might aim to double your customer base through referrals over the course of a year. Balancing short-term and long-term goals ensures that you can celebrate early successes while keeping your eye on bigger, long-term objectives.

By establishing clear rules and setting achievable goals, you're laying a solid foundation for a successful referral program. This structured approach ensures that participants know exactly what to do and what they can expect in return, which helps build trust and engagement. With clear guidelines and well-defined goals, your referral program will be well-positioned to drive growth and achieve lasting success.

CREATING INCENTIVE STRUCTURES

Designing the right incentive structure for your referral program is critical to its success. Different rewards motivate different types of referrers, so it's important to offer a variety of incentives. Monetary rewards, such as cash bonuses or gift cards, are straightforward and often highly appealing because they provide immediate, tangible benefits. Discounts on future purchases can also be effective, especially if your product or service encourages repeat business. This not only incentivizes referrals but also encourages referrers to come back and use your services again. Exclusive access to new products, events, or premium features can appeal to those who value unique experiences and feel a deeper connection to your brand.

Creating a tiered incentive system can take your referral program to the next level. By offering increasing rewards for more referrals, you can motivate participants to continue referring beyond just one or two people. For instance, you might offer a small reward for the first referral, a larger reward for the fifth, and an even bigger one for the tenth. This approach keeps participants engaged and striving for the next reward level. It's crucial, however, to balance the attractiveness of these rewards with their cost-effectiveness. You want to ensure that the incentives are appealing enough to drive participation but also sustainable for your business in the long run.

Implementing time-based goals and rewards is another strategy to encourage quick participation. Limited time offers or seasonal incentives can create a sense of urgency and prompt immediate action. For example, offering a bonus reward for referrals made within the first month of the program's launch can generate early momentum. Similarly, seasonal promotions tied to holidays or special events can boost engagement during specific periods. This approach keeps the program dynamic and encourages continuous participation throughout the year.

COMMUNICATING RULES AND GOALS

Effective communication is key to the success of your referral program. Participants need to understand the rules and goals clearly to engage fully. Best practices for communicating these elements include using straightforward language and multiple channels to reach your audience. Make sure all materials, whether brochures, emails, or website content, clearly explain how the program works, what participants need to do, and what they can expect in return. Consistency in your messaging across all platforms helps prevent confusion and ensures that everyone is on the same page.

Training and onboarding are also crucial. Providing training for referrers ensures they understand the rules and goals and feel confident in their role. This might involve a brief orientation session, detailed instructional materials, or a dedicated support team to answer questions. Onboarding new participants effectively from the start helps them feel engaged and motivated. A well-designed onboarding process can include a welcome email, a step-by-step guide to the referral process, and an overview of the rewards they can earn.

Regular updates and reminders help keep your referral program at the forefront of participants' minds. Inform them about any changes or updates to the program through newsletters, emails, and social media. Regular communication keeps participants informed and maintains their enthusiasm and participation. Highlighting success stories and milestones can also be motivating. For instance, celebrating the achievements of top referrers or announcing the program's impact on the business can inspire others to get involved.

By carefully creating your incentive structure and effectively communicating the rules and goals, you can ensure that your referral program is engaging, motivating, and aligned with your business objectives. This comprehensive approach helps build a strong foundation for a successful and sustainable referral program, driving growth and fostering loyalty among your customers.

Monitoring and Enforcing Rules

Once your referral program is up and running, monitoring and enforcing the rules is crucial to its long-term success. You need systems in place to track compliance, ensuring that all participants adhere to the program guidelines. This involves using reliable tracking tools that can accurately capture data on referrals, rewards, and participant activities. These tools not only help in maintaining transparency but also make it easier to identify any discrepancies or potential issues.

Tracking compliance isn't just about catching mistakes or abuse; it's also about ensuring that the program runs smoothly for everyone involved. By monitoring the data closely, you can quickly spot trends or patterns that might indicate a problem. For example, a sudden spike in referrals from a particular source could warrant a closer look to ensure those referrals are legitimate. Regular audits of the referral activities can help maintain the program's integrity and trustworthiness.

Enforcement strategies come into play when there are instances of non-compliance or abuse. It's important to have clear procedures for dealing with these situations to maintain the program's fairness. When participants see that rules are enforced consistently and fairly, they are more likely to trust and respect the program. If someone is found to be abusing the system, such as by creating fake referrals, there should be predefined consequences. These might range from warnings to suspension from the program, depending on the severity of the violation. Fair enforcement ensures that honest participants aren't disadvantaged by those trying to game the system.

Evaluating and Adjusting Goals

Regularly assessing your goals is essential to keep your referral program effective. Setting a schedule for these assessments helps you stay on track and make timely adjustments. By regularly reviewing performance data and participant feedback, you can gauge how well the program is meeting its objectives. This data might include metrics like the number of new customers acquired, conversion rates, and participant engagement levels.

Adjustments based on this data are key to maintaining a dynamic and responsive referral program. If you find that certain goals are not being met, or if participant feedback suggests areas for improvement, be prepared to make changes. For instance, if referrals are not converting into new customers as expected, you might need to revise your incentive structure or streamline the referral process to make it more appealing. Flexibility is crucial; the business environment and participant needs can change, and your program should adapt accordingly.

Celebrating milestones is an important aspect of keeping participants motivated. Recognizing and celebrating when key goals are met reinforces the value of their efforts and builds a sense of community and accomplishment. Whether it's reaching a significant number of referrals or achieving a high conversion rate, these milestones can be celebrated through announcements, special rewards, or public recognition. This motivates current participants to continue their efforts and encourages new participants to join the program.

By closely monitoring compliance, enforcing rules fairly, regularly assessing goals, making necessary adjustments, and celebrating achievements, you can ensure that your referral program remains effective and engaging. This comprehensive approach helps maintain the integrity of the program, adapts to changing needs, and keeps participants motivated and committed.

SUMMARY AND KEY TAKEAWAYS

In this chapter, we delved into the essential elements of establishing clear rules and achievable goals for your referral program. We began by discussing the importance of defining eligibility, setting guidelines for the referral process, and specifying reward conditions. By ensuring that everyone involved understands the rules, you create a foundation of fairness and transparency that encourages participation and trust.

We also covered the necessity of setting both short-term and long-term goals. These goals should align with your broader business objectives, whether that's increasing sales, expanding your customer base, or boosting customer loyalty. Defining key metrics to measure success, such as the number of referrals, conversion rates, and customer retention, helps you track progress and make informed adjustments.

Creating an effective incentive structure is another crucial aspect. Different rewards, such as monetary incentives, discounts, or exclusive access, can motivate different types of referrers. Designing a tiered reward system can keep participants engaged over the long term, while time-based incentives can spur quick participation. Balancing the attractiveness of rewards with cost-effectiveness ensures the sustainability of your program.

We also emphasized the importance of clear communication strategies. Ensuring that all materials clearly explain the program, providing training and onboarding for new participants, and keeping them informed through regular updates and reminders are all key to maintaining engagement and motivation.

To keep your program on track, monitoring and enforcing rules is essential. Using tracking tools to ensure compliance and having procedures in place for dealing with non-compliance or abuse helps maintain the integrity of your program. Regularly assessing your goals, making data-driven adjustments, and celebrating milestones keep your program dynamic and effective.

As you start defining rules and setting goals for your referral program, here are some practical steps to consider. Begin by clearly defining who can participate and outlining the referral process. Set specific conditions for rewards and ensure these are communicated effectively. Regularly review performance data and adjust your goals and strategies based on this feedback.

Looking ahead to the next chapter, we will explore internal processes and procedures (SOPs) for managing referral programs effectively. This will include best practices for maintaining a smooth and efficient program, ensuring all aspects are well-documented and consistently applied. Stay tuned for insights on how to streamline your operations and maximize the impact of your referral program.

5

INTERNAL PROCESSES
AND SOPS

Setting up a referral program is just the beginning. You need solid internal processes and well-documented standard operating procedures (SOPs) to ensure it runs smoothly and achieves its goals. These are the backbone of any successful referral program. They provide the structure and guidance needed to keep everything on track.

Standard operating procedures streamline the management of your referral program. Think of SOPs as the playbook for your team. They lay out each step of the process in clear, easy-to-follow instructions. This way, everyone knows exactly what to do and how to do it. With SOPs in place, there's no guesswork involved. Whether it's tracking referrals, distributing rewards, or communicating with participants, SOPs ensure that tasks are handled consistently and correctly every time.

Internal processes play a crucial role in maintaining consistency, efficiency, and quality. When you have well-defined processes, you can be confident that your referral program will operate smoothly. Consistency is key because it builds trust with your participants. They need to know that the rules are applied fairly and that rewards are given out promptly.

Efficiency is equally important. Streamlined processes save time and reduce the likelihood of errors, which can lead to participant frustration and decreased engagement.

Quality is another major benefit of solid internal processes. When everyone follows the same procedures, you can maintain a high standard of performance across the board. This means that participants have a positive experience from start to finish, which encourages them to continue referring new customers.

The importance of internal processes and SOPs can't be overstated. They are essential for the smooth operation of your referral program, ensuring that everything runs efficiently and to a high standard. By implementing clear and consistent procedures, you can build a program that achieves its goals and maintains the trust and satisfaction of your participants.

DEVELOPING STANDARD OPERATING PROCEDURES (SOPs)

Standard operating procedures, or SOPs, are the backbone of any effective referral program. They are detailed, step-by-step instructions that guide your team through every aspect of the program. The purpose of SOPs is to ensure that tasks are completed consistently and accurately, regardless of who is handling them. This consistency is crucial because it builds trust and reliability internally and with your referral program participants.

Having detailed SOPs offers numerous benefits. They provide clarity so everyone knows their responsibilities and how to execute them. This minimizes mistakes and streamlines training for new employees. Moreover, SOPs help maintain quality control, ensuring that every referral is handled the same way every time. This uniformity enhances efficiency and fosters a professional, trustworthy image for your business.

Creating SOPs involves several steps. Start by identifying all the processes that need standardization. Break down each process into individual tasks and outline these tasks in a clear, logical order. Involving key stakeholders in this creation process is essential. They bring practical insights and help ensure that the procedures are realistic and comprehensive. Their involvement also promotes buy-in, making it more likely that the SOPs will be followed consistently.

Documenting SOPs is as important as creating them. Use clear, concise language and avoid jargon that could confuse users. The goal is to make these documents accessible and easy to understand for everyone. Organize the SOPs in a logical sequence and use headings, bullet points, and numbered lists to enhance readability. Make sure these documents are easily accessible in a shared digital folder or a physical manual. Regular updates to these documents are necessary to reflect any changes in processes or feedback from users.

KEY INTERNAL PROCESSES FOR REFERRAL PROGRAMS

Effective referral tracking and management are critical to the success of your referral program. From the moment a referral is made to the point of completion, every step should be meticulously tracked. This includes recording the referrer's information, the referred individual's details, and the status of the referral at each stage. Using tools and software designed for referral tracking can significantly streamline this process. These tools provide real-time updates and reports, ensuring that no referral slips through the cracks and that all data is accurately recorded.

Reward distribution is another crucial internal process. It involves calculating the appropriate rewards, obtaining the necessary approvals, and distributing the rewards to the referrers.

This process must be timely and accurate to maintain trust and motivation among participants. Clear SOPs for reward distribution help ensure that rewards are processed efficiently and that any discrepancies are quickly addressed.

Communication and engagement are vital for keeping your referrers and participants motivated. Regular communication can include updates on the status of referrals, reminders of the rewards available, and feedback on the program's progress. Establish processes for maintaining this communication, such as monthly newsletters or automated emails. Engagement can be further enhanced by actively seeking feedback from participants and making adjustments based on their suggestions. Providing ongoing support and resources also keeps participants engaged and helps them feel valued.

You can ensure that your referral program operates smoothly and effectively by developing comprehensive SOPs and establishing robust internal processes for referral tracking, reward distribution, and communication. These steps enhance efficiency and consistency and build a solid foundation of trust and engagement with your participants. This, in turn, drives the success and growth of your referral program.

TRAINING AND ONBOARDING

Training and onboarding are vital components of a successful referral program. The first step is to ensure your staff is well-prepared. Developing comprehensive training programs for the team managing the referral program is essential. These programs should cover every aspect of the referral process, from tracking referrals to distributing rewards and communicating with participants.

Ongoing training and professional development are equally important. The business environment is constantly evolving, and so should your referral program. Regular training sessions keep your staff up-to-date with the latest best practices and any changes in the program. This continuous learning approach enhances their skills and ensures they can handle any issues that arise efficiently.

Onboarding new referrers is another critical process. When someone joins your referral program, their initial experience can set the tone for their future engagement. Start by providing a clear and concise introduction to the program, explaining how it works and what they need to do. Make sure they understand the benefits they can earn and how to track their progress.

Supporting new participants is crucial. Provide them with all the necessary resources, such as referral links, marketing materials, and access to tracking tools. Offer guidance on how to make successful referrals and be available to answer any questions they might have. A well-supported referrer is more likely to be an active and engaged participant, contributing to the overall success of your program.

Monitoring and Compliance

Ensuring adherence to SOPs is key to maintaining the integrity and effectiveness of your referral program. This involves setting up methods for monitoring compliance. Regular audits and reviews help identify any deviations from the established procedures. By consistently reviewing the process, you can spot potential issues early and address them before they become significant problems.

Addressing non-compliance promptly and fairly is essential to maintaining trust and order within the program. When someone fails to follow the rules, having clear procedures in place to handle these situations is crucial. Ensure that all participants are aware of these procedures from the start. This transparency helps in maintaining a fair environment where everyone knows the consequences of non-compliance.

Enforcing rules consistently is just as important. Participants need to see that the program is managed fairly, with everyone held to the same standards. This consistency builds trust and encourages compliance. When issues are addressed quickly and fairly, it reinforces the credibility of your program and ensures that honest participants are not disadvantaged.

By focusing on thorough training, onboarding, and diligent monitoring and compliance, you can build a referral program that runs smoothly and effectively. This structured approach ensures that everyone involved knows their role and understands the rules, creating a fair and efficient system that benefits both the business and its participants.

Continuous Improvement

Ensuring that your referral program remains effective over time requires a commitment to continuous improvement. This means regularly reviewing and updating your standard operating procedures (SOPs). By setting a schedule for these reviews, you can systematically assess how well your processes are working and identify areas for enhancement. It's important to treat this as a routine part of your program management rather than something you do only when problems arise.

During these reviews, gather feedback from everyone involved in the referral program—your staff, referrers, and even new customers. Their insights can reveal aspects of the program that may not be working as intended or could be improved. Incorporating this feedback into your SOPs helps ensure that your processes remain relevant and effective. It's about listening to the people who are directly interacting with the system and using their experiences to guide your updates.

Flexibility in your SOPs is also crucial. The business environment is constantly changing, and your referral program needs to adapt to these shifts. This could be due to new market trends, changes in customer behavior, or technological advancements. By building flexibility into your SOPs, you can quickly adjust your processes to meet new demands or opportunities. For example, if you notice a growing trend in social media referrals, you might adjust your procedures to better capture and reward these types of referrals.

Keeping your referral program dynamic and responsive ensures it remains attractive and effective. A stagnate program is unlikely to maintain participant interest or achieve its goals. Regular updates and a willingness to adapt help keep the program fresh and engaging. This proactive approach addresses current needs and anticipates future challenges, positioning your referral program for long-term success.

By committing to regular reviews and updates and maintaining the flexibility to adapt to change, you can create a referral program that evolves with your business. This ongoing improvement process ensures that your program remains efficient, effective, and aligned with your broader business objectives. A continuous cycle of assessment, feedback, and adaptation keeps your referral program robust and thriving.

Challenges and Solutions

Establishing standard operating procedures (SOPs) for a referral program can be a complex task, and it's not uncommon to encounter a few bumps along the way. One of the most frequent challenges is resistance to change. People are often accustomed to their ways of doing things, and introducing new procedures can meet with some pushback. Overcoming this requires clear communication and education. Explain the benefits of SOPs, not just for the business but for the individuals involved. Emphasize how these procedures will make their jobs easier and more efficient, ultimately leading to better results for everyone.

Another challenge is ensuring that the SOPs are detailed yet flexible enough to be practical. It's easy to fall into the trap of creating either too rigid or too vague procedures. SOPs that are too detailed can be overwhelming and stifle initiative, while those that are too broad may lead to inconsistencies. Striking the right balance involves ongoing review and refinement. Gather input from the people who use these procedures daily. Their feedback is invaluable for identifying what works and what doesn't.

Consistency is also a common hurdle. Ensuring that everyone adheres to the SOPs can be difficult, especially in larger organizations. Regular training and reminders are essential. Make sure that the importance of following the SOPs is part of the company culture. Lead by example and recognize and reward compliance. This reinforces the value of SOPs and encourages others to follow suit.

Documentation is another area where businesses often struggle. Poorly documented SOPs can lead to confusion and errors. Invest time in creating clear, concise, and accessible documents. Use simple language and break down complex processes into manageable steps. Visual aids like flowcharts and diagrams can also help clarify procedures.

Practical advice for avoiding these pitfalls includes starting with a pilot program. Implement the SOPs on a smaller scale first, gather feedback, and make necessary adjustments before rolling them out company wide. This approach allows you to identify and address issues early on.

Additionally, it's important to stay flexible. Business environments and needs change, and your SOPs should be able to adapt. Regularly review and update your procedures to ensure they remain relevant and effective. Encourage a culture of continuous improvement, where feedback is actively sought and valued.

In summary, while establishing SOPs can be challenging, these obstacles can be overcome with clear communication, regular training, consistent documentation, and a flexible approach. By addressing these challenges head-on, you can develop robust SOPs that enhance the efficiency and effectiveness of your referral program, contributing to its long-term success.

SUMMARY AND KEY TAKEAWAYS

This chapter delved into the essential role of internal processes and standard operating procedures (SOPs) in managing a successful referral program. We started by defining SOPs and exploring their purpose. SOPs are detailed, step-by-step instructions that ensure consistency, efficiency, and quality across all aspects of your referral program. They serve as a playbook that guides your team, eliminates ambiguity, and enhances trust among participants.

We discussed the process of creating SOPs, emphasizing the importance of involving key stakeholders. Their input is crucial in developing practical and comprehensive procedures. We also covered best practices for documenting SOPs, highlighting the need for clarity, accessibility, and ease of use. Well-documented SOPs are essential for smooth onboarding and training, ensuring everyone knows their responsibilities and how to execute them effectively.

Key internal processes were also explored in detail. We looked at the importance of robust referral tracking and management, efficient reward distribution, and regular communication with participants. Each of these processes is critical for keeping your referral program running smoothly and maintaining participant engagement.

Training and onboarding were highlighted as vital components. Effective training programs ensure that your staff is well-prepared to manage the referral program, while a thorough onboarding process for new referrers helps set the right expectations and provides the necessary support for success.

Monitoring and compliance are essential for maintaining the integrity of your program. Regular audits, reviews, and clear procedures for handling non-compliance ensure that the rules are followed consistently and fairly. This consistency builds trust and reliability, both internally and with your participants.

We also discussed the importance of continuous improvement. Regular reviews and updates to SOPs, incorporating feedback, and adapting to changes in the business environment keep your referral program dynamic and responsive. This ongoing refinement process ensures your program remains effective and aligned with your business goals.

To put these concepts into action, here are some practical steps for developing and implementing SOPs for your referral program. Start by identifying all the key processes that need standardization. Involve your team in creating detailed, clear procedures and document them thoroughly. Provide regular training and updates to ensure everyone is on the same page. Monitor compliance and be ready to make adjustments as needed.

Looking ahead to the next chapter, we will focus on measuring the success of your referral program and making data-driven decisions. This will include identifying key metrics, analyzing performance data, and using insights to refine and improve your program. By understanding how to effectively measure success, you can ensure that your referral program continues to drive growth and achieve its objectives. Stay tuned for a deeper dive into the analytics that will help you optimize your referral strategy.

6

DOCUMENTING PROCESSES

Documenting processes is fundamental to running a successful and scalable referral program. It ensures that every team member understands their role and the steps they need to follow, leading to a more efficient and effective operation. Without clear documentation, you risk inconsistency, miscommunication, and errors that can undermine your program's success.

The importance of documenting processes cannot be overstated. When processes are well-documented, tasks are performed consistently and to a high standard. This consistency is crucial in maintaining the integrity and reliability of your referral program. Each referral must follow the same steps to ensure fairness and transparency, from initiation to reward distribution. Clear documentation helps achieve this by providing a reference that everyone can follow, reducing the chances of deviation from the established procedures.

Moreover, documentation plays a vital role in training and onboarding new staff. It is a comprehensive guide that new employees can use to quickly understand their responsibilities. This accelerates the onboarding process and ensures that new team members can hit the ground running. They don't have to rely on sporadic training sessions or verbal instructions that might vary each time. Instead, they have access to a consistent resource outlining every process step.

Documentation also ensures continuity. In any business, staff turnover is inevitable. Without proper documentation, the departure of a key team member can lead to the loss of crucial knowledge and disrupt the referral program. Documented processes capture this knowledge and make it easily transferable. When a new person steps into the role, they can refer to the documentation to understand the established practices and continue the work without missing a beat.

Documenting processes is essential for the success and scalability of a referral program. It maintains consistency, enhances training and onboarding, and ensures continuity. By committing to thorough and clear documentation, you lay a strong foundation for a referral program that can grow and thrive, regardless of changes in personnel or other challenges. This foundational step is key to creating a sustainable and effective referral system that delivers consistent results.

Benefits of Documenting Processes

Documenting processes brings numerous benefits to your referral program. The most significant advantages are consistency and quality control. When you have well-documented processes, everyone follows the same steps, ensuring that tasks are performed to a high standard each time. This uniformity is crucial in maintaining the program's integrity. Participants know what to expect, and team members can perform their duties without confusion. It eliminates the guesswork, making sure that every referral is handled with the same level of care and precision.

Another key benefit is in training and onboarding new staff. Documented processes make these activities much more efficient. When new employees join the team, they don't have to rely solely on verbal instructions or sporadic training sessions. Instead, they can refer to the comprehensive guides that outline every aspect of their role. This speeds up the onboarding process and helps new hires become productive more quickly. They clearly understand their responsibilities and the steps they need to follow, which reduces the learning curve and helps them integrate smoothly into the team.

Operational efficiency is also greatly enhanced through clear documentation. When everyone knows exactly what to do and how to do it, operations run more smoothly. There's less room for misunderstandings or errors, which can be costly and time-consuming to correct. Clear documentation streamlines workflows, ensuring that tasks are completed accurately and promptly. This not only saves time but also improves your team's overall productivity.

Knowledge retention is another critical benefit of documenting processes. In any business, staff turnover is inevitable. Without proper documentation, the departure of a key team member can result in a significant loss of institutional knowledge. Documented processes capture this knowledge, making it easily transferable. New team members can quickly get up to speed by referring to the documentation, ensuring that the knowledge and expertise of the previous employees are preserved. This continuity is vital for maintaining the smooth operation of your referral program.

TYPES OF DOCUMENTATION

Several types of documentation can support your referral program. Process documentation provides detailed descriptions of each process involved in the program. This includes everything from how referrals are tracked to how rewards are distributed. These detailed descriptions ensure that every aspect of the program is covered and that all team members are on the same page.

Procedural guides offer step-by-step instructions for specific tasks and activities. These guides break down each task into manageable steps, making it easy for team members to follow along. Whether it's how to input a referral into the system or how to handle a customer inquiry, procedural guides provide the necessary details to perform tasks accurately and efficiently.

Training manuals are comprehensive guides used for training new staff or referrers. These manuals cover all the essential information that new hires need to know. They provide a structured approach to training, ensuring that all new employees receive the same information and training. This consistency helps to standardize the onboarding process and ensures that all team members are adequately prepared for their roles.

Checklists and templates are practical tools that help ensure all steps are followed correctly and consistently. Checklists can be used to verify that all necessary steps have been completed for each referral, while templates provide standardized formats for common documents and communications. These tools help maintain consistency and reduce the likelihood of errors, ensuring that all aspects of the referral program are handled correctly.

By leveraging these different types of documentation, you can create a robust framework that supports your referral program's success. Each type of documentation plays a specific role in ensuring that processes are clear, consistent, and easily transferable, contributing to the overall efficiency and effectiveness of the program.

STEPS TO DOCUMENTING PROCESSES

Documenting processes starts with identifying the key processes that need documentation. You must determine which aspects of your referral program are critical to its success and require clear guidelines. This involves looking at every step in your program, from how referrals are collected to how rewards are distributed. Once you've identified these key processes, the next step is visually mapping them out. Creating flowcharts or diagrams can help you and your team see the entire process from start to finish. These visual aids provide a clear picture of each step involved and how they connect, making it easier to identify any gaps or inefficiencies.

When it comes to writing clear descriptions of these processes, simplicity is key. The goal is to make sure that anyone can understand and follow the instructions. Use straightforward language and avoid jargon that might confuse the reader. Be concise but comprehensive, ensuring that every necessary detail is included without overwhelming the reader with unnecessary information. Think of it as writing a recipe—each step should be clear and easy to follow.

Collaborating with your team is crucial during this documentation process. Your team members directly involved in these processes can provide valuable insights and ensure the documentation is accurate. Involve them in reviewing the drafts and ask for their feedback. This helps capture the nuances of each process and ensures that the documentation is practical and usable.

BEST PRACTICES FOR EFFECTIVE DOCUMENTATION

It's important to use simple language to create effective documentation. The goal is to make the information accessible to everyone, regardless of their familiarity with the technical details. Avoiding jargon and using plain language ensures that all team members, from new hires to experienced staff, can easily understand the documentation.

Organizing the information in a logical, user-friendly format is another critical aspect. Structure your documents so that they flow naturally from one section to the next. Use headings, subheadings, and bullet points to break up the text and make it easier to read. This not only helps in finding information quickly but also makes the document less intimidating.

Incorporating visual aids such as diagrams, flowcharts, and images can significantly enhance understanding. Visual aids help to illustrate complex processes and make them easier to grasp. They provide a quick reference that can often communicate more effectively than text alone. For example, a flowchart can show the steps of a referral process at a glance, making it easier for team members to follow along.

Regular reviews and updates are essential to keep your documentation current. Business processes can change over time, and your documentation needs to reflect these changes. Set a schedule for regular reviews and solicit feedback from your team to identify any areas that need updating. This ensures that your documentation remains relevant and useful.

By following these steps and best practices, you can create comprehensive and effective documentation for your referral program. This documentation will serve as a valuable resource for your team, helping to maintain consistency, improve efficiency, and ensure the success of your referral program.

TOOLS AND TECHNOLOGIES FOR DOCUMENTATION

The right tools and technologies can make a significant difference when documenting processes. Documentation software provides a robust platform for creating, storing, and managing your process documents. Many options are available, each with its own set of features designed to make documentation easier and more efficient. Some software offers templates to help you get started, while others provide advanced features like real-time collaboration and automated workflows. The goal is to find a tool that fits your needs and makes the documentation process as smooth as possible.

Collaboration platforms are another essential tool. These platforms allow multiple stakeholders to contribute to and review the documentation. Tools like Google Workspace, Microsoft Teams, and Slack facilitate real-time collaboration, making it easy for team members to share their insights and feedback. This collaborative approach ensures that the documentation is comprehensive and incorporates input from those who are directly involved in the processes.

Version control systems are crucial for managing updates and revisions. These systems help you keep track of changes made to the documentation, ensuring that everyone is working with the most current information. They allow you to revert to previous versions if necessary and provide a clear audit trail of changes. This is particularly important in maintaining the accuracy and reliability of your documentation over time.

Implementing Documentation

Once you have your documentation in place, the next step is to train your staff on how to use it effectively. It is crucial to educate your team on the importance of documented processes and how to refer to them in their daily tasks. This training can be part of onboarding for new employees and ongoing professional development for existing staff. It ensures that everyone understands the value of the documentation and knows how to access and use it correctly.

Integrating documentation into daily operations is another key aspect. The goal is to make process documentation a natural part of your workflows. Encourage your team to refer to the documentation regularly and make it easily accessible.

This can be achieved by linking the documentation within your team's tools and platforms, such as project management software or intranet systems. By embedding documentation into everyday tasks, you ensure that it is consistently used and becomes an integral part of how your business operates.

Monitoring the usage and effectiveness of your documentation is essential for continuous improvement. Regularly assess how well the documentation is being utilized and its impact on your operations. This can involve surveys, feedback sessions, and performance metrics. Are your team members finding the documentation helpful? Is it reducing errors and improving efficiency? Use this feedback to make necessary adjustments and updates, ensuring that your documentation remains relevant and effective.

In conclusion, leveraging the right tools and technologies can significantly enhance your documentation efforts. Training your staff and integrating documentation into daily operations ensures that it is used effectively. Regular monitoring and feedback help maintain its relevance and impact. By focusing on these aspects, you can create a robust documentation system that supports your referral program's success and scalability.

Summary and Key Takeaways

This chapter explored the critical importance of documenting processes for your referral program. We began by understanding why process documentation is essential. It ensures consistency, improves training and onboarding, enhances operational efficiency, and preserves institutional knowledge. These elements are the backbone of a scalable and successful referral program.

We discussed the various benefits of having well-documented processes. Consistency and quality control are achieved when everyone follows the same procedures, ensuring high standards are maintained across the board. Documented processes also streamline training and onboarding, allowing new staff to quickly understand their roles and responsibilities. This efficiency is crucial for smooth operations and helps reduce misunderstandings or errors. Moreover, having clear documentation helps retain and transfer institutional knowledge, making it easier to manage transitions when team members leave or join.

Next, we covered the types of documentation that can support your referral program. Process documentation includes detailed descriptions of each step involved, while procedural guides provide step-by-step instructions for specific tasks. Training manuals are comprehensive resources for new hires, and checklists and templates ensure that all steps are followed consistently.

To create effective documentation, we outlined the steps involved. Identifying key processes, mapping them out visually, writing clear descriptions, and involving stakeholders are all crucial steps in this process. Using simple language, organizing information logically, incorporating visual aids, and regularly reviewing and updating the documentation are best practices that ensure clarity and usability.

We also explored the tools and technologies that can aid in documenting processes. Documentation software, collaboration platforms, and version control systems play a vital role in creating, sharing, and maintaining your documents. These tools help streamline the documentation process and ensure that the most current information is always accessible.

Implementing documentation involves training your staff on how to use and refer to the documented processes. Integrating this documentation into daily operations ensures it becomes a natural part of your workflow. Monitoring usage and effectiveness allows you to assess how well the documentation is being utilized and make necessary adjustments.

To implement these concepts, here are some practical steps to start documenting your processes. Begin by identifying the key processes that need documentation. Create detailed descriptions and visual aids to map out each step. Involve your team to gather insights and ensure accuracy. Use the right tools and technologies to facilitate the documentation process and update it regularly.

The next chapter will focus on training and onboarding new staff and referrers. We will explore strategies for effectively integrating new team members into your referral program and ensuring they are well-equipped to contribute to its success. Stay tuned for practical advice on building a strong, knowledgeable team that can drive your referral program forward.

7

TIME MANAGEMENT AND EFFICIENCY

Effective time management is crucial for the success of any referral program. When we manage our time well, we can focus on the tasks that drive results and move the program forward. Time is a finite resource, and how we choose to allocate it can make the difference between a thriving referral program and one that struggles to gain traction.

Efficient time management contributes to productivity in several ways. By organizing and prioritizing our tasks, we ensure that the most important activities are completed first. This approach helps us avoid the common pitfall of spending too much time on tasks that don't add significant value to the program. It also reduces stress and improves our ability to meet deadlines, which is essential for maintaining the momentum of the referral program.

The role of efficiency in referral programs is equally important. Efficiency means doing things right with the least amount of wasted effort and resources. When our processes are efficient, we can handle more referrals without increasing our workload proportionately. This scalability is vital for growth. For instance, if we can streamline the process of tracking and rewarding referrals, we free up time to focus on recruiting new referrers or improving customer engagement.

Efficiency also impacts the overall success of the referral program. An efficient program can provide a seamless experience for both the referrers and the new customers. This positive experience encourages more participation and fosters loyalty. Moreover, efficient operations can lead to cost savings, which can then be reinvested into the program to enhance its offerings or expand its reach.

Mastering time management and efficiency is foundational to the success and scalability of a referral program. By prioritizing tasks, streamlining processes, and minimizing waste, we can create a program that not only meets but exceeds its goals. This approach ensures that we make the most of our resources and position the program for sustained growth and success.

IDENTIFYING TIME WASTERS

Running a referral program efficiently means being vigilant about how we spend our time. Time wasters are activities that eat up our hours without contributing meaningful value to our program. Identifying these time wasters is the first step towards better time management.

Common time wasters in referral programs often include administrative tasks that could be automated, excessive meetings without clear agendas, and responding to non-urgent emails throughout the day. For example, manually tracking referrals when software could do it more accurately and quickly is a classic time waster. Similarly, holding long meetings that do not lead to concrete decisions or actions can drain valuable time that could be spent on more productive activities.

To assess our current time management practices, we must closely examine our daily routines. One effective technique is to keep a weekly time log, recording every task we perform and how long it takes. This exercise helps us see patterns and identify where time is being spent inefficiently. Another method is periodically reviewing our workflows and asking critical questions: Are there redundant steps? Are we spending too much time on low-priority tasks? This honest assessment is crucial for uncovering inefficiencies and making necessary adjustments.

STRATEGIES FOR EFFECTIVE TIME MANAGEMENT

Once we have identified the time wasters, we can implement strategies to manage our time more effectively. Prioritization is key. We need to focus on tasks that impact our referral program's success most.

One effective method for prioritizing tasks is the Eisenhower Matrix. This tool helps us categorize tasks based on their urgency and importance. Both urgent and important tasks go into one quadrant and should be done immediately. Important but not urgent tasks should be scheduled for later, while urgent but less important tasks can be delegated. Finally, tasks that are neither urgent nor important can often be eliminated. This matrix helps us focus our efforts where they matter most and avoid getting bogged down by less critical activities.

Time blocking is another powerful technique. We can create a structured schedule that minimizes distractions by dedicating specific blocks of time to particular tasks. For example, we might set aside the first hour of the day to respond to emails, followed by a two-hour block to work on referral program strategies. This approach helps ensure that important tasks get the focused attention they need and reduces the temptation to multitask, which can decrease productivity.

We can ensure that our referral program runs smoothly and efficiently by identifying time wasters and implementing effective time management strategies like prioritization and time blocking. These practices help us make the most of our time, focus on what truly matters, and ultimately drive the success of our referral efforts.

STREAMLINING PROCESSES

Streamlining processes is essential to run a successful referral program. Automating repetitive tasks is one of the most effective ways to do this. Often, many small, routine tasks consume significant amounts of time. Identifying these tasks is the first step towards automation. For example, tracking referral submissions, sending confirmation emails, and generating reports can all be automated. We can free up valuable time by using tools like customer relationship management (CRM) software or specialized referral program platforms. Automation saves time and reduces the risk of human error, ensuring tasks are completed accurately and consistently.

Another critical aspect of streamlining processes is delegating responsibilities. Delegation is about assigning the right tasks to the right people. You must recognize that you don't have to do everything yourself. Delegating tasks to team members improves efficiency, empowers them, and fosters a sense of ownership. To delegate effectively, clearly define the task, explain its importance, and provide any necessary resources or guidance. Regular check-ins can help ensure that the task is on track without micromanaging. By trusting your team and leveraging their skills, you can focus on higher-level strategic activities that drive the program forward.

TOOLS AND TECHNOLOGIES FOR TIME MANAGEMENT

Leveraging the right tools and technologies can significantly enhance time management. Project management software is a game-changer when it comes to organizing tasks and managing time efficiently. Tools like Asana, Trello, or Monday.com allow you to create task lists, set deadlines, and track progress in real time. These platforms offer features such as task assignments, priority settings, and reminders, which help ensure that everyone stays on track and that nothing falls through the cracks.

Productivity apps are another valuable resource. Apps like Todoist, Evernote, or Microsoft OneNote can help you keep track of your to-do lists, set reminders, and organize your thoughts. These apps are designed to help both individuals and teams stay productive by providing a central place to manage tasks and deadlines. Features like tagging, color-coding, and project folders make it easy to keep everything organized and accessible.

Communication platforms play a crucial role in enhancing coordination and efficiency. Tools like Slack, Microsoft Teams, or Zoom facilitate seamless communication among team members. These platforms support instant messaging, video conferencing, file sharing, and integration with other productivity tools. Effective communication is essential for coordinating tasks, sharing updates, and resolving issues quickly. By using these tools, teams can collaborate more effectively, even when working remotely.

Automating repetitive tasks and delegating responsibilities are key strategies for streamlining processes and improving efficiency. Leveraging project management software, productivity apps, and communication platforms can enhance time management and ensure your referral program runs smoothly. By integrating these tools and strategies into your workflow, you can maximize productivity, reduce stress, and achieve better outcomes for your referral program.

BEST PRACTICES FOR MAINTAINING EFFICIENCY

Maintaining efficiency in a referral program requires setting realistic goals. Goals need to be achievable and aligned with our time management strategy. Setting overly ambitious goals can lead to burnout and frustration, while goals that are too easy might not push us enough to achieve our full potential. The key is to find a balance. For example, if our goal is to increase the number of referrals, we need to consider how much time and resources we have available to support this increase. Breaking down larger goals into smaller, manageable tasks can help us stay on track and see progress without feeling overwhelmed.

Regularly reviewing our time management practices is crucial. It's easy to fall into a routine and assume that our current methods are working. However, taking the time to reflect on our practices can reveal inefficiencies and areas for improvement. Set aside time, perhaps monthly or quarterly, to review how we're spending our time. Are there tasks that consistently take longer than expected? Are there new tools or techniques that could help us be more efficient? We can continuously improve our workflow and stay adaptable to changing circumstances by making regular adjustments.

Minimizing distractions is another essential practice for maintaining efficiency. In today's world, distractions are everywhere—emails, social media, phone calls, and even office chatter. Creating a distraction-free work environment helps us focus better and finish more quickly. One technique is to designate specific times for checking emails and messages rather than responding to them as they come in. Setting boundaries, such as using noise-canceling headphones or putting up a "do not disturb" sign, can also help create a focused workspace. Another method is to use apps or tools that block distracting websites during work hours. By actively managing our environment and habits, we can significantly reduce distractions and enhance our productivity.

Setting realistic goals, regularly reviewing and adjusting our time management practices, and minimizing distractions are key strategies for maintaining efficiency. By implementing these best practices, we can ensure that our referral program operates smoothly and effectively, allowing us to achieve our objectives and foster sustained growth. These habits not only improve our productivity but also create a more focused and motivated team ready to tackle any challenges that come our way.

Challenges and Solutions

Managing time effectively isn't without its challenges. One common issue is the constant influx of tasks and distractions that can derail even the best-laid plans. For instance, unexpected meetings or urgent emails can throw off your schedule and make it difficult to focus on high-priority tasks. I've found that one solution to this problem is to build flexibility into my schedule. Setting aside blocks of time specifically for handling unforeseen tasks allows me to stay on top of my priorities without feeling overwhelmed when something unexpected comes up.

Another challenge is procrastination, which can be a significant time-waster. It's easy to put off tasks that seem daunting or less enjoyable, but this only leads to stress and a backlog of work. To overcome procrastination, I break tasks into smaller, more manageable steps. This approach makes the work seem less intimidating and helps me maintain a steady pace. Setting deadlines for each step, even if they are self-imposed, can also provide the motivation needed to stay on track.

Distractions are another major obstacle. These interruptions can significantly reduce productivity, whether it's the constant ping of notifications or colleagues stopping by to chat. To combat this, I've adopted a few strategies. Turning off non-essential notifications during work hours and creating a quiet workspace can help maintain focus. Additionally, communicating with colleagues about dedicated "focus times" can minimize interruptions and create a more productive environment for everyone.

A more subtle challenge is the tendency to overcommit. It's easy to say yes to every request, especially when trying to be helpful or eager to take on new opportunities. However, overcommitting can lead to burnout and a drop in the quality of work. Learning to prioritize and sometimes say no is essential. Evaluating each new task or project against current priorities helps in making informed decisions about what to take on and what to delegate or defer.

Summary and Key Takeaways

In this chapter, we explored various aspects of time management and efficiency, focusing on their importance for the success of a referral program. We started with identifying common time wasters and assessing current time management practices to pinpoint inefficiencies. Strategies for effective time management, such as prioritization techniques, the Eisenhower Matrix, and time blocking, were discussed to help structure tasks and enhance productivity.

We then moved on to streamlining processes by automating repetitive tasks and delegating responsibilities. Using the right tools and technologies, such as project management software, productivity apps, and communication platforms, further supports efficient time management. Best practices like setting realistic goals, regularly reviewing and adjusting practices, and minimizing distractions are crucial for maintaining efficiency.

In tackling common challenges, we identified practical solutions such as building flexibility into schedules, breaking tasks into manageable steps, and creating distraction-free work environments. These strategies help overcome obstacles and pave the way for sustained productivity and program growth.

To put these concepts into action, start by evaluating your current time management practices and identifying areas for improvement. Implement prioritization techniques and time management tools that best fit your needs. Regularly review and adjust your practices to stay efficient and avoid common pitfalls.

Looking ahead to the next chapter, we will focus on building and maintaining strong relationships with referrers and new customers. Strong relationships are the backbone of a successful referral program, and we'll explore strategies for nurturing these connections to ensure long-term success. Stay tuned for insights on fostering loyalty and engagement within your referral network.

8

GROWTH AND SCALING

G rowth and scaling are not just goals; they are vital for the long-term success of any referral program. Without a clear strategy for growth, a referral program can stagnate, limiting its potential and failing to contribute meaningfully to the business's broader objectives. Scaling ensures the program can handle increased demand without sacrificing quality or efficiency.

Growth strategies are essential because they lead to increased revenue and market presence. When a referral program grows, it taps into a broader network of potential customers. Each new referrer brings in new contacts, exponentially expanding the program's reach. This expanded reach translates to more leads, more conversions, and, ultimately, higher revenue. Moreover, as the program grows, it reinforces the brand's presence in the market. A robust referral program can turn loyal customers into brand advocates who actively promote the business to their networks, further solidifying its market position.

Scaling, however, ensures that it remains sustainable and manageable as the program grows. It involves refining processes, leveraging technology, and optimizing resources to handle an increased volume of referrals without compromising on the quality of service. Effective scaling means that the referral program can smoothly accommodate growth, with systems in place to manage more participants and transactions efficiently.

Growth and scaling are interconnected. Growth brings new opportunities and revenue, while scaling ensures that these opportunities are managed effectively, keeping the program robust and efficient. This combination of growth and scaling is crucial for maintaining the momentum of the referral program and ensuring it continues to deliver value both to the business and its customers. By focusing on these aspects, businesses can create a referral program that expands their customer base and enhances their market presence and revenue streams.

Preparing for Growth

Before we can set our referral program on a path to growth, it's essential to take a step back and assess its current state. Evaluating our referral program involves a thorough look at what's working well and what could use some improvement. Are we seeing consistent participation from our referrers? Are the incentives attractive enough? Are we efficiently tracking and rewarding referrals? Identifying these strengths helps us understand our foundation, while pinpointing areas for improvement allows us to address potential roadblocks before they hinder our growth efforts.

Once we have a clear picture of our current capabilities, we will set growth objectives. Clear, achievable goals are crucial. These objectives should be ambitious enough to drive progress but realistic enough to be attainable. For instance, we might aim to increase the number of active referrers by 20 percent over the next quarter. Aligning these growth objectives with our overall business goals ensures that the referral program supports the broader company strategy. If our business goal is to enter a new market, our referral program should focus on recruiting referrers and acquiring customers from that market.

STRATEGIES FOR GROWTH

Expanding our referral network is a key strategy for growth. We can implement various techniques to recruit more referrers. One effective approach is to leverage existing relationships. Our current satisfied customers are our best advocates. Encouraging them to refer friends and family can significantly boost our network. Additionally, we can tap into professional networks and partnerships. Collaborating with other businesses that complement ours can open doors to new potential referrers who already have established trust within their communities.

Enhancing our incentive programs is another powerful strategy. People are motivated by rewards, and we can attract more participants by revising and improving our incentives. Offering tiered rewards can make the program more appealing. For example, referrers who bring in five new customers might receive a larger reward than those who refer just one. Special promotions, such as limited-time bonus rewards, can also create excitement and urgency, driving more referrals during specific periods.

Improving customer engagement is crucial for both referrers and referred customers. Engaged referrers are more likely to continue participating, and engaged new customers are more likely to become repeat customers. Personalized communication plays a significant role in this. By tailoring our messages to address our audience's specific needs and interests, we can create a more meaningful connection. Targeted marketing campaigns can help maintain this engagement. For instance, sending regular updates and success stories can motivate referrers and remind them of the benefits they can gain by participating in the program.

Preparing for growth requires evaluating our current capabilities thoroughly and setting clear, aligned objectives. Strategies for growth include expanding our referral network, enhancing incentive programs, and improving customer engagement. Focusing on these areas can create a robust referral program that drives significant growth and supports our overall business goals.

LEVERAGING TECHNOLOGY FOR SCALING

Technology is a powerful ally when it comes to scaling a referral program. One of the most effective ways to harness this power is through automation. Automating repetitive tasks can streamline our referral processes, making them more efficient and less prone to human error. For instance, automation tools can handle everything from sending confirmation emails to tracking referral progress and distributing rewards. This saves time and ensures that each step in the referral process is executed consistently.

Integrating referral software with our existing business systems is another critical step. This integration allows different parts of our business to work together seamlessly. For example, by linking our referral software with our customer relationship management (CRM) system, we can comprehensively view each customer's journey from referral to conversion. This integration helps maintain a smooth flow of information, which is crucial for managing the referral program and providing excellent customer service.

Data analytics plays a crucial role in scaling our referral program. We can track performance and identify growth opportunities by analyzing the data collected from our referral activities. Metrics such as referral rates, conversion rates, and customer retention give us valuable insights into how well our program is performing. Using these insights, we can make data-driven decisions to refine our strategies. For instance, if we notice that certain types of incentives lead to higher referral rates, we can adjust our incentive structure accordingly.

Maintaining Quality and Consistency

Maintaining quality and consistency becomes even more important as our referral program scales. High standards must be upheld to ensure that the program remains effective and trustworthy. Implementing quality control measures, such as regular audits and feedback mechanisms, helps us monitor the program's performance and identify areas for improvement. These audits can reveal discrepancies or issues that need to be addressed, ensuring that every aspect of the referral program meets our established standards.

Regular feedback from referrers and customers is also invaluable. This feedback provides insights into their experiences with the program, highlighting what works well and what needs improvement. By actively seeking and acting on this feedback, we can continuously improve the program, ensuring it remains relevant and effective.

Training and support are essential components of maintaining quality as the program scales. Providing ongoing training ensures that referrers understand how to effectively participate in the program and maximize their success. This training can include tutorials, webinars, and easy-to-follow guides that explain the referral process and best practices.

Support resources are equally important. Developing a robust support system helps referrers overcome any challenges they might encounter. This might include a dedicated support team to answer questions, a comprehensive FAQ section on the program's website, and regular updates to keep referrers informed about any changes or new opportunities within the program.

In conclusion, leveraging technology through automation and integration and utilizing data analytics for decision-making are key strategies for scaling a referral program. Maintaining quality and consistency through regular audits, feedback, training, and support ensures that the program remains effective and trusted as it grows. By focusing on these areas, we can build a scalable referral program that drives significant growth and continues delivering value to our business and customers.

Overcoming Challenges in Scaling

Scaling a referral program is not without its hurdles. As the program grows, we often face a series of challenges that can hinder progress if not addressed properly. One common obstacle is resource constraints. As we bring in more referrers and customers, we need additional resources to manage the increased workload. This might include more staff, enhanced technology, or greater financial investment. Without proper planning, these demands can strain our existing resources, leading to inefficiencies and potential program breakdowns.

Operational complexities also pose significant challenges. As the program scales, managing the various components becomes increasingly complicated. Coordinating communication between referrers, tracking numerous referrals, and ensuring timely reward distribution require robust systems and processes. Any lapse in these areas can result in dissatisfaction among participants and undermine the program's credibility.

It's essential to adopt a strategic approach to overcome these challenges. Planning and preparation are key. We need to anticipate the additional resources required and ensure they are in place before scaling efforts begin. This might involve securing additional funding, hiring more staff, or investing in more advanced technology to handle the increased volume.

Implementing robust systems is another critical solution. Automated tools can streamline many of the processes involved in managing a referral program, reducing the burden on our team and minimizing the risk of human error. For example, automating the tracking of referrals and the distribution of rewards ensures that these tasks are completed accurately and efficiently, regardless of the program's size.

Learning from businesses that have successfully scaled their referral programs can provide valuable insights and best practices. Take, for instance, a company that managed to double its referral rates by integrating a sophisticated CRM system. This integration allowed them to track every referral meticulously, ensuring no leads were lost and rewards were distributed promptly. Their experience highlights the importance of having the right technology in place to support growth.

Another example is a business that overcame resource constraints by gradually scaling its program. Instead of trying to expand rapidly, they set incremental goals and scaled in phases. This approach allowed them to manage resources effectively and address any operational issues at each stage before moving to the next. This phased approach ensured that the program grew sustainably and without overwhelming the existing infrastructure.

Scaling a referral program successfully requires a proactive approach to potential obstacles. By anticipating resource needs, implementing robust systems, and learning from others' experiences, we can navigate the complexities of scaling effectively. These strategies help overcome challenges and ensure that our referral program continues to thrive and deliver significant value as it grows.

Learning from Challenges

Every scaling journey comes with its own set of challenges. However, these challenges offer valuable lessons that can help refine our strategies and strengthen our referral programs. Let's look at some real-world examples of programs that faced significant hurdles during scaling and how they overcame them.

Consider a tech startup that aimed to rapidly expand its referral program to capture a larger market share. They initially struggled with resource constraints, particularly in customer support. As the volume of referrals increased, so did the number of customer inquiries and issues. This overwhelmed their small support team, leading to delays and frustration among customers and referrers.

To address this, they implemented an automated support system. They integrated a chatbot that could handle common queries and direct more complex issues to human agents. This system significantly reduced the burden on their support staff, allowing them to manage the increased volume effectively. Additionally, they hired and trained a few more support agents, anticipating future growth. Combining automation with strategic hiring ensured that customer support remained efficient and responsive, even as the program scaled.

Another example is an e-commerce company that struggled with maintaining the quality and consistency of its referral rewards. As their program grew, discrepancies in reward distribution began to emerge, causing dissatisfaction among referrers. The root of the problem was their outdated tracking system, which couldn't handle the increased data accurately.

The company invested in a more robust referral management software that seamlessly integrates with its existing systems. This new software provided real-time tracking and reporting, ensuring that all referrals were accurately recorded and rewards were distributed promptly. They also established regular audits to monitor the system's performance and address any issues proactively. By upgrading their technology and implementing quality control measures, they maintained the integrity of their referral program and regained the trust of their referrers.

These examples allow us to draw several practical insights for avoiding common pitfalls. First, anticipating and planning for resource needs is crucial. As your program scales, ensure that you have the necessary support systems and personnel in place. Second, investing in the right technology can make a significant difference. Robust systems for tracking, managing, and supporting your referral program are essential for handling increased volume without compromising on quality. Finally, regular audits and feedback mechanisms are invaluable for maintaining high standards and addressing issues before they escalate.

Summary and Key Takeaways

This chapter explored the importance of growth and scaling for the long-term success of a referral program. We discussed the need for thorough preparation, including assessing current capabilities and setting clear growth objectives. We delved into strategies for expanding the referral network, enhancing incentive programs, and improving customer engagement.

Leveraging technology was highlighted as a crucial factor for scaling, with automation and data analytics playing key roles in streamlining processes and making informed decisions. We also emphasized the importance of maintaining quality and consistency through regular audits, feedback, and ongoing training and support.

By learning from challenges faced by other programs, we gained practical insights into overcoming obstacles and avoiding common pitfalls. These examples underscored the need for strategic planning, robust systems, and proactive problem-solving.

To implement these concepts, start by evaluating your referral program's current state and setting realistic growth goals. Implement strategies to expand your network, enhance engagement, and leverage technology to support your scaling efforts. Regularly review and adjust your practices to ensure quality and efficiency.

The next chapter will focus on measuring success and making data-driven decisions for continuous improvement. We will explore key metrics to track, how to analyze performance data, and ways to refine your strategies based on these insights. This approach will ensure that your referral program remains effective and continues to deliver value as it grows.

9

BUILDING THE RIGHT TEAM

Building a strong team is the cornerstone of any successful referral program. A capable and cohesive team doesn't just execute tasks—they drive the program forward, ensuring it meets and exceeds its goals. When you have the right people in the right roles, everything flows more smoothly, from managing day-to-day operations to implementing long-term strategies.

A strong team brings a wealth of diverse skills and perspectives. Each member contributes their unique expertise, whether it's in marketing, customer support, data analysis, or IT. This diversity enriches the program and ensures that all aspects are covered comprehensively. For example, a marketing specialist might develop compelling campaigns to attract new referrers, while a data analyst tracks these campaigns' effectiveness and identifies areas for improvement. The referral program operates like a well-oiled machine when these roles work together seamlessly.

Moreover, a cohesive team fosters a positive work environment. When team members communicate well and collaborate effectively, it boosts morale and enhances productivity. Clear communication helps in setting and achieving common goals. Everyone knows their responsibilities and how their work contributes to the program's overall success. This shared sense of purpose can be incredibly motivating, driving team members to go above and beyond.

The right team also plays a crucial role in driving growth. Skilled team members can identify expansion opportunities, whether it's reaching out to new markets or refining the incentive structure to attract more participants. They bring creativity and innovation, essential ingredients for staying competitive in a dynamic market. Furthermore, a strong team can adapt to challenges and changes, ensuring the program remains resilient and responsive.

In essence, the success of a referral program hinges on its team. With capable, motivated individuals working together towards a common goal, the program can achieve significant growth and deliver outstanding results. As we delve deeper into building and managing the right team, it's clear that investing in people is investing in the program's future. A strong team is not just an asset—it's the foundation for the entire referral program.

Identifying Key Roles

Building an effective referral program starts with identifying the key roles that will drive its success. The heart of any strong program is a dedicated program manager. This person oversees the entire operation, ensuring that all parts work together smoothly. They are responsible for setting goals, tracking progress, and making strategic decisions to improve the program. The program manager needs excellent leadership skills, a strategic mindset, and the ability to manage multiple tasks simultaneously.

A marketing specialist is crucial for attracting new referrers and engaging existing ones. They design and implement marketing campaigns, create promotional materials, and manage social media outreach. The ideal marketing specialist is creative, has a keen understanding of digital marketing, and knows how to analyze campaign performance to make data-driven improvements.

Customer support representatives are the frontline of the program, handling inquiries from referrers and referred customers. They need to be knowledgeable about the referral process and able to resolve issues quickly and efficiently. Strong communication skills and a customer-first attitude are essential for this role.

A data analyst plays a key role in tracking the referral program's performance. They collect and analyze data to identify trends, measure success, and recommend improvements. The data analyst should have strong analytical skills, be proficient in data analysis tools, and have the ability to interpret complex data into actionable insights.

Lastly, an IT specialist ensures that all technological aspects of the referral program run smoothly. They manage the referral software, troubleshoot technical issues, and ensure data security. The IT specialist needs to be tech-savvy, detail-oriented, and proactive in maintaining and improving the technology infrastructure.

RECRUITING TOP TALENT

Once we have identified the key roles, the next step is to attract top talent to fill these positions. Attracting qualified candidates starts with crafting compelling job descriptions that clearly outline the responsibilities and qualifications for each role. Job boards, social media platforms, and industry networks are excellent tools for reaching a broad audience. Posting on specialized job boards that cater to marketing, customer service, data analysis, and IT professionals can also help target the right candidates.

Utilizing industry networks and employee referrals can also yield high-quality candidates. The best hires often come from within our professional circles or recommendations from trusted colleagues. Engaging with industry associations, attending networking events, and participating in online forums can connect us with potential candidates who are already established in their fields.

We identify the best fit for our team in the interviewing and selection process. Effective interviewing techniques involve asking questions that reveal not just the candidates' skills and experience but also their problem-solving abilities, teamwork, and cultural fit. Behavioral interview questions that focus on past experiences can provide insights into how candidates handle real-world challenges.

When evaluating candidates, it's important to consider both their technical qualifications and their potential to grow within the organization. Look for individuals who are not only skilled but also show enthusiasm for the role and a willingness to learn. Making final decisions should involve input from multiple team members to ensure a well-rounded evaluation of each candidate's fit for the team and the program.

In summary, identifying key roles and responsibilities, attracting top talent through strategic recruitment, and conducting thorough interviews are foundational steps in building a strong team for our referral program. By focusing on these areas, we can assemble a team that is well-equipped to drive the program's success and contribute to the overall growth of our business.

BUILDING A COHESIVE TEAM

Creating a cohesive team is essential for the success of our referral program. Teamwork and collaboration don't just happen; they must be fostered through intentional efforts. Promoting teamwork starts with creating an environment where everyone feels valued and heard. One effective technique is holding regular team meetings where members can share updates, discuss challenges, and brainstorm solutions together. These meetings should be structured but also allow for open dialogue, encouraging everyone to contribute their ideas.

Clear communication is the cornerstone of a collaborative team. Setting team goals that everyone understands and is committed to is crucial. When everyone knows what they're working towards, staying aligned and motivated is easier. Regularly revisiting these goals and tracking progress keeps the team focused and accountable.

Team-building activities are also vital for strengthening team bonds. These activities don't have to be elaborate. Simple exercises like team lunches, brainstorming sessions, or problem-solving workshops can make a big difference. For example, organizing a monthly team lunch where everyone shares their successes and challenges can foster a sense of camaraderie. Participating in volunteer activities as a team can also build stronger connections and give everyone a shared sense of purpose outside of work.

The benefits of regular team-building efforts are numerous. A positive work environment where team members feel connected and supported leads to higher morale, increased productivity, and reduced turnover. When people enjoy working together, they are more likely to go the extra mile to help each other and achieve common goals.

TRAINING AND DEVELOPMENT

Bringing new hires on board smoothly is crucial for maintaining the momentum of our referral program. A comprehensive onboarding process is the first step in integrating new team members. This process should include a thorough introduction to the company's culture, values, and the specific goals of the referral program. New hires should be given all the necessary resources, such as access to relevant software, training manuals, and a clear outline of their responsibilities. Pairing new team members with a mentor or a buddy can also help them acclimate faster and feel more comfortable in their new role.

Continuous professional development is just as important as onboarding. The business landscape is always evolving, and our team needs to evolve with it. Providing opportunities for ongoing learning keeps our team's skills sharp and their knowledge current. This can be achieved through workshops, courses, webinars, and industry conferences. Encouraging team members to pursue certifications or further education in their fields enhances their skills and shows that we value their growth and career development.

Offering diverse training programs tailored to the needs of different roles within the team ensures that everyone can benefit. For example, marketing specialists might need advanced courses in digital marketing trends, while customer support representatives could benefit from conflict resolution and communication skills training. By investing in our team's development, we're investing in the long-term success of our referral program.

Fostering team collaboration and providing ongoing training and development are essential strategies for building a strong, cohesive team. Through clear communication, team-building activities, comprehensive onboarding, and continuous learning opportunities, we create an environment where our team can thrive and drive the success of our referral program.

RETAINING TOP TALENT

Retaining top talent is crucial for the sustained success of our referral program. Creating a positive work culture is one of the most effective ways to keep our best employees. A supportive and engaging work environment motivates employees to stay committed and perform at their best. We can foster this type of culture by promoting open communication, where everyone feels free to share ideas and feedback. Regular team meetings and open-door policies can facilitate this.

Recognition and rewards are also vital in maintaining a positive work culture. Celebrating achievements, whether big or small, can boost morale and make employees feel valued. This could be as simple as acknowledging someone's effort during a meeting or offering more formal rewards like bonuses or extra time off. By recognizing hard work and dedication, we show our team that we appreciate their contributions, fostering loyalty and motivation.

Providing clear paths for career advancement within the organization is another key strategy for retaining top talent. Employees need to see a future for themselves in the company. This means offering opportunities for promotion and professional growth. Regularly discussing career aspirations with team members can help identify these opportunities. Encouraging employees to set professional development goals and providing the resources to achieve them—such as funding for courses or time off for attending workshops—demonstrates our commitment to their growth. Employees who see that their career development is a priority are more likely to stay with the company long-term.

MANAGING TEAM PERFORMANCE

Managing team performance effectively requires setting clear performance metrics. Key performance indicators (KPIs) help us track how well the team and individual members are doing. These metrics should align with the overall goals of the referral program. For example, KPIs might include the number of new referrals generated, the conversion rate of referrals to customers, or customer satisfaction scores. Regularly reviewing these metrics can gauge our progress and identify areas that need improvement.

Providing feedback and coaching is essential for helping team members grow and improve. Regular performance reviews offer a structured opportunity to discuss each employee's strengths and areas for development. Constructive feedback should be specific and actionable, focusing on behaviors and outcomes rather than personal attributes. Coaching techniques, such as asking open-ended questions and actively listening, can help team members reflect on their performance and develop their own solutions. This approach supports individual growth and builds a culture of continuous improvement.

Retaining top talent involves creating a positive work culture with recognition and rewards and offering clear career growth opportunities. Managing team performance requires setting aligned performance metrics and providing regular, constructive feedback and coaching. These practices ensure that our team remains motivated, engaged, and capable of driving the success of our referral program. Focusing on these areas creates an environment where our team members can thrive and contribute to the program's long-term goals.

Learning from Challenges

Every team faces challenges, and how we respond to these obstacles defines our success. I recall a team struggling with communication and collaboration, leading to missed deadlines and decreased morale. The issue stemmed from unclear roles and responsibilities, which created confusion and frustration among team members. To address this, we initiated a series of team-building exercises and workshops focused on improving communication skills. We also held a series of meetings to clarify roles and establish clear, achievable goals. Over time, these efforts paid off, and the team began working more cohesively, meeting their deadlines, and achieving higher productivity.

Another example involved a team dealing with the rapid scaling of a referral program. As the program grew, the existing processes and tools became inadequate, causing significant stress and burnout. We tackled this by investing in new technology to automate repetitive tasks and streamline workflows. Additionally, we brought in new hires to distribute the workload more evenly. We also implemented regular check-ins to ensure team members felt supported and could voice concerns. These changes led to a more balanced workload, improved efficiency, and a more satisfied team.

From these experiences, several practical insights emerge for managing and improving team dynamics. Clear communication is essential. Ensure every team member understands their role and how their work contributes to the overall goals. Regular team-building activities can strengthen relationships and foster a collaborative environment. It's also crucial to be proactive in identifying and addressing issues. Encourage team members to share their challenges openly and be prepared to make adjustments to processes and tools as needed. Finally, support your team through growth phases by providing the necessary resources and training to handle increased demands effectively.

Summary and Key Takeaways

In this chapter, we delved into the critical aspects of building and managing a strong team for a referral program. We began by emphasizing the importance of a capable and cohesive team in driving the program's success. Identifying key roles such as Program Manager, Marketing Specialist, Customer Support

Representative, Data Analyst, and IT Specialist ensures that all necessary functions are covered.

We discussed strategies for recruiting top talent, including crafting compelling job descriptions and utilizing various recruitment channels. Building a cohesive team involves fostering collaboration, clear communication, and regular team-building activities. Training and development during onboarding and ongoing professional growth are vital for keeping the team skilled and motivated.

Retaining top talent requires creating a positive work culture, recognizing achievements, and offering clear career growth opportunities. Managing team performance involves setting aligned performance metrics and providing regular feedback and coaching. Learning from challenges faced by other teams offers practical insights into improving team dynamics and overcoming obstacles.

To implement these concepts, start by identifying the key roles needed for your referral program and recruiting the best candidates. Foster a collaborative environment, provide comprehensive training, and recognize and reward your team's efforts. Regularly review and adjust your strategies to ensure continuous improvement and success.

CONCLUSION

As we conclude this book, it's valuable to take a moment to reflect on the journey we've embarked on together. Throughout the chapters, we've explored the essential components of building and maintaining a successful referral program.

We began by understanding the importance of referral programs and how they can serve as a powerful tool for business growth. We delved into the intricacies of setting up such a program, identifying key roles, and recruiting top talent to drive its success. From there, we explored how to build a cohesive team, emphasizing the necessity of clear communication and collaborative efforts.

Our discussion on training and development highlighted the need for comprehensive onboarding and continuous professional growth. This naturally led us to strategies for retaining top talent by fostering a positive work culture and providing clear career advancement paths.

We didn't shy away from the challenges, either. We looked at common scaling issues and gained practical insights into what works and what doesn't, allowing us to adapt and refine our strategies.

The overarching theme has been the importance of structured processes, from documenting standard operating procedures to leveraging technology for automation and data-driven decision-making. Each chapter built upon the previous one, reinforcing the idea that a successful referral program is not a standalone effort but an integrated part of a larger business strategy.

Importance of a Strong Referral Program

The benefits of a well-implemented referral program are numerous and far-reaching. Over the long term, a strong referral program can significantly boost customer acquisition. New customers brought in through referrals are often more likely to convert and become loyal, repeat clients. This enhanced customer loyalty is a cornerstone of sustainable business growth, providing a steady stream of revenue and stability.

Moreover, referral programs are cost-effective. Compared to traditional marketing strategies, referrals typically require less financial investment while yielding high returns. The trust inherent in a personal recommendation often translates into a higher conversion rate, meaning your marketing dollars go further.

Strategically, a robust referral program aligns perfectly with broader business goals. It supports growth by continuously bringing in new customers and fostering deeper relationships with existing ones. This alignment ensures that your referral program isn't just an add-on but a vital component of your overall business strategy, driving sustainable growth and resilience.

As we wrap up our exploration of referral programs, remember that the true power of these programs lies in their ability to integrate seamlessly into your business's fabric. By leveraging the strategies, insights, and best practices discussed in this book, you can build a referral program that achieves immediate goals and supports long-term success and growth.

ACTIONABLE STEPS FOR IMPLEMENTATION

Implementing a successful referral program begins with a clear plan and defined goals. Start by identifying the core objectives of your program. Are you looking to increase customer acquisition, boost sales, or enhance brand loyalty? Once your goals are set, you need to map out the steps to achieve them. This involves identifying your key stakeholders who will drive and support the program. Engage these stakeholders early, ensuring they understand the program's value and are committed to its success.

Next, focus on the practical aspects of launching your referral program. Develop a compelling value proposition that encourages participation. Why should someone refer your business to others? Make sure the incentives are attractive and clear. Utilize various marketing channels to promote your referral program—email campaigns, social media, and your website are great starting points.

As your program gains traction, scaling becomes the next critical step. Leverage technology to handle increased participation and streamline operations. Automation tools can manage referral tracking, reward distribution, and communication, freeing your team to focus on strategy and engagement. However, growth should not come at the expense of quality. Maintain a consistent experience for all participants by regularly auditing your processes and ensuring your technology infrastructure can handle the load.

Continuous improvement is essential for keeping your referral program effective and relevant. Regularly review performance metrics and gather feedback from participants. Use this data to refine your strategies, update incentives, and address any issues. This iterative approach helps you stay responsive to changing market conditions and participant needs, ensuring your program remains attractive and effective.

OVERCOMING COMMON CHALLENGES

Every referral program will face its share of challenges. Identifying and addressing these issues promptly can mean the difference between success and failure. Common obstacles include low participation rates, tracking inaccuracies, and managing increased operational demands as the program scales.

To overcome low participation rates, make sure your value proposition is compelling and well-communicated. Participants need to see the clear benefits of referring others. If tracking inaccuracies are a problem, investing in reliable referral software can help. These tools provide accurate, real-time data and reduce the risk of errors that can undermine trust in your program.

Managing operational demands requires a balance between technology and human oversight. Automation can handle repetitive tasks, but a dedicated team should oversee the program's overall health, addressing issues and ensuring a seamless participant experience.

Flexibility and innovation are crucial in adapting to changing market conditions. Be prepared to tweak your referral program as needed. This might involve updating your incentive structures, exploring new marketing channels, or incorporating participant feedback into your strategy. Staying flexible allows your program to evolve with your business and the market, ensuring long-term relevance and effectiveness.

CONCLUSION

Launching and managing a referral program is a dynamic process that requires careful planning, strategic growth, and continuous improvement. By starting with clear goals, leveraging technology for scaling, and staying flexible to adapt to changes, you can create a referral program that meets and exceeds your business objectives.

In this journey, remember that challenges are growth opportunities. By addressing issues head-on and staying open to innovation, you can build a robust referral program that drives sustainable growth and customer loyalty. As you implement these strategies, keep in mind the broader impact on your business—every referral is a testament to your brand's value and a step toward long-term success.

CLOSING REMARKS

I want to take a moment to express my gratitude to you, the readers. Your dedication to improving your referral programs is commendable, and I appreciate the time and effort you've invested in this journey. Your success is the goal of this book, and I hope the insights and strategies shared here have been valuable to you.

I invite you to engage with this community of referral program enthusiasts. Share your experiences, feedback, and success stories. Your insights can help others on their path to creating successful referral programs, and together, we can foster a community of continuous improvement and mutual support.

Thank you once again for your time and interest. Here's to the growth and success of your referral programs and the exciting future that lies ahead.

Work Less and Make More Money Than Ever Before

Take your business to the next level
with a fresh perspective.

Jason Miller's insights show you exactly how to break
through plateaus and achieve big profits.

Go beyond your expectations and
see what's possible for your business.

jetlaunch.link/SABdiscover

About the Author

Jason Miller is an accomplished business leader with over thirty years of experience, renowned for his expertise in hyper company growth, scaling, and strategic and operational implementation. He founded the Strategic Advisor Board (SAB) in 2017 and served as its Senior Global Council Member, overseeing its global operations and team capabilities. In addition to his primary role at SAB, Jason holds multiple chair positions across various companies and nonprofits. He has built more than twenty-four companies from scratch since 2001 and is dedicated to crafting sustainable business models emphasizing leadership responsibility, strategy, and accountability.

Known for his no-excuses approach and nicknamed "The Bull," Jason has advised thousands of global leaders. He has been recognized as a foremost expert in consulting for creating scalable business models, particularly for small and mid-market companies. His focus extends to fostering a positive company culture, enhancing staff retention, and deepening customer loyalty, believing that a clear vision and purpose are essential for impactful business. As a veteran, Jason is committed to serving veteran-owned companies and provides pro bono services to veteran organizations as part of a five-year plan.

Jason holds an MBA from Trident University and credits the "school of hard knocks" for his doctorate in practical experience. He is affiliated with numerous prestigious organizations that impact business globally, such as the American Club Association, Leigh Steinberg Academy, Forbes Council, and Entrepreneur Magazine Leadership Council. A lifetime member of the American Legion, Disabled American Veterans, and Veterans of Foreign Wars, Jason lives in Boulder, Colorado, with his family. He focuses on professional development and business strategy to serve his clients better.

www.ingramcontent.com/pod-product-compliance
Lightning Source LLC
Chambersburg PA
CBHW050526190326
41458CB00045B/6720/J